Management of Pharmaceutical Household Waste

LIMITING ENVIRONMENTAL IMPACTS OF UNUSED OR EXPIRED MEDICINE

OECD

BETTER POLICIES FOR BETTER LIVES

This document, as well as any data and map included herein, are without prejudice to the status of or sovereignty over any territory, to the delimitation of international frontiers and boundaries and to the name of any territory, city or area.

The statistical data for Israel are supplied by and under the responsibility of the relevant Israeli authorities. The use of such data by the OECD is without prejudice to the status of the Golan Heights, East Jerusalem and Israeli settlements in the West Bank under the terms of international law.

Note by Turkey
The information in this document with reference to "Cyprus" relates to the southern part of the Island. There is no single authority representing both Turkish and Greek Cypriot people on the Island. Turkey recognises the Turkish Republic of Northern Cyprus (TRNC). Until a lasting and equitable solution is found within the context of the United Nations, Turkey shall preserve its position concerning the "Cyprus issue".

Note by all the European Union Member States of the OECD and the European Union
The Republic of Cyprus is recognised by all members of the United Nations with the exception of Turkey. The information in this document relates to the area under the effective control of the Government of the Republic of Cyprus.

Please cite this publication as:
OECD (2022), *Management of Pharmaceutical Household Waste: Limiting Environmental Impacts of Unused or Expired Medicine*, OECD Publishing, Paris, https://doi.org/10.1787/3854026c-en.

ISBN 978-92-64-45290-9 (print)
ISBN 978-92-64-65186-9 (pdf)
ISBN 978-92-64-31506-8 (HTML)
ISBN 978-92-64-81794-4 (epub)

Foreword

Pharmaceuticals are an important element of medical and veterinary practice, with beneficial effects on human and animal health, food production and economic welfare. Despite these many benefits, pharmaceuticals are a concern when they are discharged into the environment.

Pharmaceutical household waste from expired or unused medicine does not only offer zero therapeutic benefit, but contributes to environmental pollution when disposed of via improper routes. When flushed in household drains, these medicines can enter freshwater systems. Illegal dumping and landfills present further pathways of possible environmental leakage of medicines disposed in municipal solid waste.

The adverse environmental impacts of improper disposal of pharmaceutical household waste are threefold. First, evidence is growing that certain pharmaceuticals affect ecosystems. Observed impacts on wildlife include mortality, changes to physiology, behaviour or reproduction. For instance, laboratory and field tests show that traces of oral contraceptives can cause the feminisation of fish and amphibians, and residues of psychiatric drugs can alter fish behaviour. In addition, improper disposal of antibiotics can contribute to the development of antimicrobial resistant bacteria. Second, unused or expired medicines present a possible public health risk of accidental or intentional misuse and poisoning if extracted from waste bins. Third, unused or expired medicines constitute wasted healthcare resources and economic losses. These risks are likely to be exacerbated in the future, as pharmaceutical usage is projected to continue to increase, due to demographic, epidemiological and lifestyle changes, such as an ageing and growing population, the rise of chronic health conditions and the availability of inexpensive generic treatments and changes in clinical practice.

OECD's legal instruments provide a strong rationale for policy intervention in this area. The *OECD Council Recommendation on the Environmentally Sound Management (ESM) of Waste* calls for Adherents to implement policies and/or programmes to ensure that waste be managed in an environmentally sound and economically efficient manner. In addition, the *OECD Council Recommendation on Water* calls for Adherents to prevent, reduce and manage all sources of water pollution, in surface and ground waters and related coastal ecosystems, while paying attention to pollutants of emerging concern. Preventing pharmaceutical household waste and ensuring the effective collection and environmentally sound treatment of unavoidable waste is thus an important policy objective.

This report outlines measures to reduce the amount and impact of unused or expired medicine. Policymakers will find in this report inspiration and pragmatic support to translate ambitions into actions that improve health and protect the environment.

Acknowledgements

This report is an output of the OECD Environment Policy Committee (EPOC) and its Working Party on Resource Productivity and Waste (WPRPW). It has been authored by Frithjof Laubinger, with support in conceptualisation, analysis, methodology and supervision by Peter Börkey, and analysis, reviewing and editing by Maarten Dubois. The work on this report was conducted under the overall supervision of Shardul Agrawala, Head of the Environment and Economy Integration Division of the OECD's Environment Directorate.

The Secretariat gratefully acknowledges the contributions of the delegates of the Working Party on Resource Productivity and Waste (WPRPW).

The authors express gratitude to those who contributed to the preparation and development of this report through the provision of their time, expertise and experience, including: Luis Rhodes Baiao (Association of the European Self-Medication Industry [AESGP]); Thierry Moreau Defarges (Cyclamed); Helena Bladh and Katja Murray (GSK); Delphine Lagourgue (Health Products Stewardship Association, Canada); Jan De Belie (Pharmaceutical Group of the European Union [PGEU]); Maikel Batelaan (Pharmafilter); Jelmer Faber (PharmaSwap); Kristin Aldred Cheek and Scott Cassel (Product Stewardship Institute, United States); Charlotte Bekker (Radboud University Nijmegen, The Netherlands); Miguel Vega (SIGRE); Luís Figueiredo (VALORMED); and Brigit van Soest-Segers (Vereniging Innovatieve Geneesmiddelen, The Netherlands). Appreciation is extended to Andrew Brown and Nikhil Varghese who provided valuable input and reviewed comments and Aziza Perriere (all OECD Environment Directorate) who provided editorial assistance.

Table of contents

6 |

Tables

Figures

Boxes

Follow OECD Publications on:

http://twitter.com/OECD_Pubs

http://www.facebook.com/OECDPublications

http://www.linkedin.com/groups/OECD-Publications-4645871

http://www.youtube.com/oecdilibrary

http://www.oecd.org/oecddirect/

Abbreviations

API	Active pharmaceutical ingredients
CPR	Collective producer responsibility
CSO	Combined Sewer Overflow
DEA	US Drug Enforcement Administration
EPR	Extended Producer Responsibility
FDA	US Food and Drug Administration
HPSA	Health Products Stewardship Association Canada
IPR	Individual Producer Responsibility
MSW	Municipal Solid Waste
NatRUM	Australian National Return of Unused Medicines scheme
OTC	Over-the-counter drugs
PANS	Pharmacy Association of Nova Scotia
PRO	Producer Responsibility Organization
SAMHSA	US Substance Abuse and Mental Health Services Administration
UBA	Umweltbundesamt (German Environment Agency)
UEM	Unused or expired medicines
USD	US Dollar
WWTP	Wastewater treatment plants

Executive summary

Pharmaceuticals are essential for human and animal health, but they become an environmental concern when their residues enter the environment. Pharmaceutical pollution can occur when residues are excreted after consumption or when unused or expired medicine is discarded improperly.

A significant share of household medicine becomes waste, and the volumes are steadily increasing due to trends in pharmaceuticals consumption

Household medicine can become waste for numerous reasons. Non-adherence, early recovery, therapy changes or prescription and purchasing errors can all lead to medicine remaining unused or expiring in households. Estimates of the share of household medication becoming waste vary from 3% to as high as 50%. In France, it was estimated that households disposed of 17 600 tonnes of unused or expired medicine in 2018, equivalent to 260 g per capita.

Demographic, epidemiological and lifestyle changes such as an ageing and growing population, the rise of chronic health conditions, the availability of inexpensive generic treatments and changes in clinical practice have led to increased pharmaceutical prescription and usage in OECD countries. As a consequence, the amount of unused medicine that becomes waste is also increasing, which makes their environmentally sound management ever more important.

Improper disposal of unused or expired medicine is widespread and results in significant environmental contamination and public health risks

Medicines flushed via sinks and toilets enter sewage waters and risk leaking into freshwater systems. Conventional wastewater treatment plants are not designed to remove pharmaceuticals, resulting in emissions into waterbodies in unchanged or metabolised form. Depending on the removal efficiency of the conventional wastewater treatment plants, some pharmaceutical residues are removed to a limited extent and collected in the sewage sludge. These may still enter environmental systems, when sewage sludge is applied on land for agricultural use ("landspreading") or composting, both common practices in most OECD countries.

Pharmaceuticals disposed of in municipal solid waste can also enter the environment. When mixed municipal solid waste is landfilled, pharmaceutical residues risk leaching into the environment if leachate is not collected and treated properly.

The implications of improper disposal of unused or expired medicine are threefold. First, certain pharmaceuticals have been proven to cause adverse effects to ecosystems when entering environmental systems, including increased mortality in aquatic species and changes to physiology, behaviour or reproduction. The discharge of antibiotics can also lead to mutations in animals and the development of antimicrobial resistant bacteria. Second, there is a possible public health risk of accidental or intentional misuse and poisoning if unused medicine is extracted from public or private waste bins. Third, unused pharmaceuticals represent wasted healthcare resources and economic losses.

Policy interventions aimed at preventing and collecting unused medicines, as well as better consumer information can help to avoid and better manage pharmaceutical household waste

Various policy interventions can be taken across the lifecycle including source-directed, user-orientated and waste management measures, to prevent medicine waste and reduce environmental leakage.

First, prevention measures such as improved disease prevention, personalised and precision medicine or better dimensioning of packaging sizes can help avoid pharmaceutical waste. A study in the Netherlands estimated that approximately 40% of pharmaceutical waste through unused or expired medicines could be prevented. Marketplaces for and redistribution of unused close-to-expiry date medicines can also improve the matching of supply and demand and prevent wastage. Resale and re-dispensing of unused medicines is still a niche, due to concerns regarding counterfeits, quality assurance and consequent legal restraints, but a number of initiatives exist.

Nevertheless, fully eliminating unused medicines is difficult. For instance, some patients may recover more rapidly than foreseen, change their treatment or not adhere to prescribed treatments. Patients may also preventively stock over-the-counter drugs, which expire before being completely utilised. Ensuring proper collection and disposal of these unused or expired medicines is thus indispensable.

Collection and disposal of unavoidable pharmaceutical waste needs to be customised to the national context and local challenges. Where there is a risk that medicine disposed in mixed waste can leach or be misused, separate collection is recommended to reduce environmental and public health impacts. Extended producer responsibility schemes have shown to be an effective approach to organise environmentally sound separate collection and treatment. The four OECD countries with highest collection ratios (i.e. France, Sweden, Portugal and Spain) have an extended producer responsibility scheme in place with full and harmonised national coverage and with collection points at pharmacies. Alternative approaches such as publicly financed take-back schemes can also be effective but do not implement the polluter pays principle.

Finally, limited awareness of consumers about proper disposal routes and drug take-back schemes weakens their impact in many countries. In Latvia, 60% of respondents admitted to not being aware of how to dispose of unused or expired medicine properly. A survey conducted in the Netherlands concluded that 17.5% were unaware that liquid medicines should not be flushed. In order to increase the awareness of citizens about proper disposal routes and/or the existence of drug take-back schemes, governments should develop, or mandate producer responsibility organisations to set up well-focused communication campaigns. In particular, liquids, ointments and creams tend to be discarded improperly, which highlights that further information campaigns or behavioural nudges would be beneficial in many countries.

Additional approaches that can also lead to increased awareness and behavioural change include: special instructions for appropriate disposal routes that appear on the outer packaging of medicinal products or in the information leaflet, nudges such as 'challenges' or 'saving accounts' to return medication to pharmacies or product ecolabelling to inform consumer choices. Awareness and informative tools for health professionals can also help to strengthen environmental considerations in prescription practices and disseminate the risk of inappropriate disposal routes among the population.

1 Introduction

This chapter introduces the issue and provides on overview of the structure of the report.

Demographic, epidemiological and lifestyle changes such as an ageing population, the rise of chronic health conditions and the availability of inexpensive generic treatments have been key drivers for increased pharmaceutical usage in OECD countries (OECD, 2021[1]). About 4 000 active pharmaceutical ingredients (APIs) are being administered worldwide in prescription medicines, over-the-counter therapeutic drugs and veterinary drugs (Burns et al., 2018[2]). Over the past two decades, per-capita consumption of lipid-modifying agents has increased by a factor of nearly four and per-capita consumption of anti-diabetic and anti-depressants has doubled (OECD, 2021[1]).

Pharmaceuticals are essential for human and animal health but become an environmental concern if their residues enter freshwater systems. Aquatic pollution can occur when residues are excreted after consumption or when unused or expired medicine (UEM) is discarded inappropriately. Pharmaceutical residues are now ubiquitous in surface water, groundwater and seawater worldwide (OECD, 2019[3]). Pharmaceuticals have been found in 75 different countries and 771 substances have been detected in the environment, sometimes above pollution thresholds (German Environment Agency, 2019[4]).

The health and environmental impacts of freshwater contamination vary strongly across the types of pharmaceuticals. Some pharmaceuticals have an endocrine function, meaning that they affect the hormone system. Endocrine-disrupting pharmaceuticals have been found to have adverse effects on wildlife, even at very low concentrations. For example, steroidal hormones in contraceptive pills have been proven to impair reproduction of exposed fish populations and psychiatric drugs were found to alter fish behaviour (Brodin et al., 2013[5]; Nash et al., 2004[6]). Furthermore, the discharge of antibiotics in water bodies can be linked to the spread of pathogenic organisms that are resistant to antimicrobials, causing an alarming public health threat worldwide (BIO Intelligence Service, 2013[7]; Ferreira da Silva et al., 2007[8]; OECD, 2018[9]).

Unused pharmaceuticals also pose a health risk due to misuse and (un)intentional poisonings. In the US, seven out of ten people who abuse prescription drugs get them from friends and family (Hughes et al., 2016[10]) and drug overdose has become the leading cause of accidental death in the US, before car accidents (Trust for America's Health, 2015[11]). According to the 2018 National Survey on Drug Use and Health, 9.9 million US citizens misused controlled prescription drugs (SAMHSA, 2019[12]).

Additionally, UEM represents a wasted healthcare resource. Several studies estimate the costs of unused or expired drugs to be in the order of billions of USD (Law et al., 2015[13]; Bach et al., 2016[14]; Trueman et al., 2010[15]).

Various policy interventions can be taken across the lifecycle to reduce the environmental and health impacts of UEM. Whilst waste prevention is critical, fully eliminating unused medicines is difficult. For instance, patients may recover more rapidly than foreseen, change their treatment or not adhere to the prescribed treatments. Patients may also preventively stock over-the-counter drugs, which expire before being completely utilised. Proper collection and disposal of unavoidable UEM is therefore indispensable.

This report reviews pharmaceutical waste management systems in different OECD countries and is structured as follows. Chapter 2 outlines the dominant sources and pathways of pharmaceuticals entering the environment. Chapter 3 reviews estimated amounts and disposal practices of UEM in different OECD countries. Chapter 4 provides an overview of the current policy landscape for pharmaceutical waste management and reviews a selection of waste collection schemes. Chapter 5 concludes the analysis with policy recommendations and considerations.

2 Sources and entry-pathways of pharmaceuticals into the environment

This chapter describes the major sources and entry-pathways of pharmaceuticals into the environment and the environmental implications.

1.1. Sources

Pharmaceuticals and their metabolites can enter the environment during production, consumption and disposal (Kümmerer, 2009[16]; Lapworth et al., 2012[17]). The following are the key sources.

2.1.1. Households

Excreted pharmaceuticals after consumption make up the largest source of household emissions. Between 30-90% of the oral doses of pharmaceuticals are generally excreted either as original compound or as metabolite. Creams and ointments washed off skin may also end up in wastewater (BIO Intelligence Service, 2013[7]).

Medicine that expires or remains unused is a significant waste stream and when disposed of improperly can also contribute to household emissions. An estimated 3-50% of pharmaceuticals become waste (Chapter 3, Section 3.1). Unused or expired medicines that are disposed of via bathroom sinks and toilets is one source of UEM emission to wastewater. Disposal of UEM via municipal solid waste destined for final disposal in landfills can also lead to leaching of pharmaceutical residues over time, if this leachate is not captured and treated appropriately (Masoner et al., 2014[18]).

Box 2.1. Definition of household disposal and final disposal

Literature and legislation use the term "disposal" for two different practices, at different parts of the waste value chain:

- *Household disposal* refers to the disposal practices of unused or expired drugs by consumers and households (e.g. flushing, household bin, return to collection points, dumping)
- *Final disposal* refers to the treatment practices of municipal solid waste in a given country (e.g. landfilling or incineration of collected UEM)

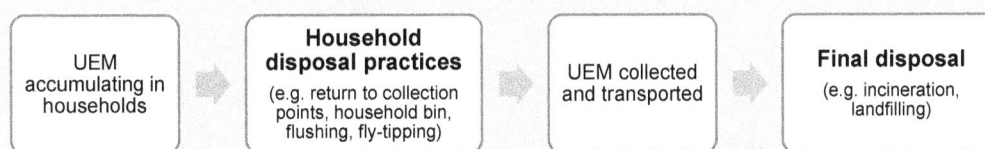

UEM accumulating in households → **Household disposal practices** (e.g. return to collection points, household bin, flushing, fly-tipping) → UEM collected and transported → **Final disposal** (e.g. incineration, landfilling)

2.1.2. Hospitals

Hospitals, healthcare services and long-term care facilities are point sources of pharmaceutical substances going into the sewage network. Whilst the pharmaceutical loading of their wastewater is high, their contribution to the overall pharmaceutical contamination of wastewater varies per type of medicine. According to studies in Sweden and Norway, contributions lie around 1-3% for most pharmaceuticals, as much medication prescribed in hospitals is consumed at home and advanced care increasingly takes place in private homes (Thomas et al., 2007[19]; Larsson and Lööf, 2016[20]).[1] Another study estimates the contribution of hospitals to the environmental load in the EU at about 10% (Kümmerer and Hempel, 2010[21]). In Denmark's Copenhagen region, an estimated 24% of the total antibiotic load originates from hospitals. For hospital specific substances such as cytostatic or endocrine medicines or contrast media, the contribution can be higher (BIO Intelligence Service, 2013[7]).

2.1.3. Pharmaceutical production

Industrial chemical residues from manufacturing APIs and pharmaceuticals can enter the water cycle through direct discharge (i.e. industrial wastewater) and indirect discharge (in case of leakage). Globally, this source is considered low compared to the amount excreted by patients, but local hot spots can exist.

2.1.4. Veterinary pharmaceuticals

Pharmaceuticals for veterinary use, aquaculture and agriculture present an important source of pharmaceuticals entering the environment. Similar to human consumption, 30-90% of the pharmaceutical consumed by animals is excreted as original compound or metabolite in animal faeces. Veterinary pharmaceuticals in aquaculture directly enter waterbodies, whereas the common reuse of livestock manure leads to entry pathways into the soil, surface water and groundwater.[2]

Figure 2.1. Main sources and pathways of human pharmaceutical residues to the environment

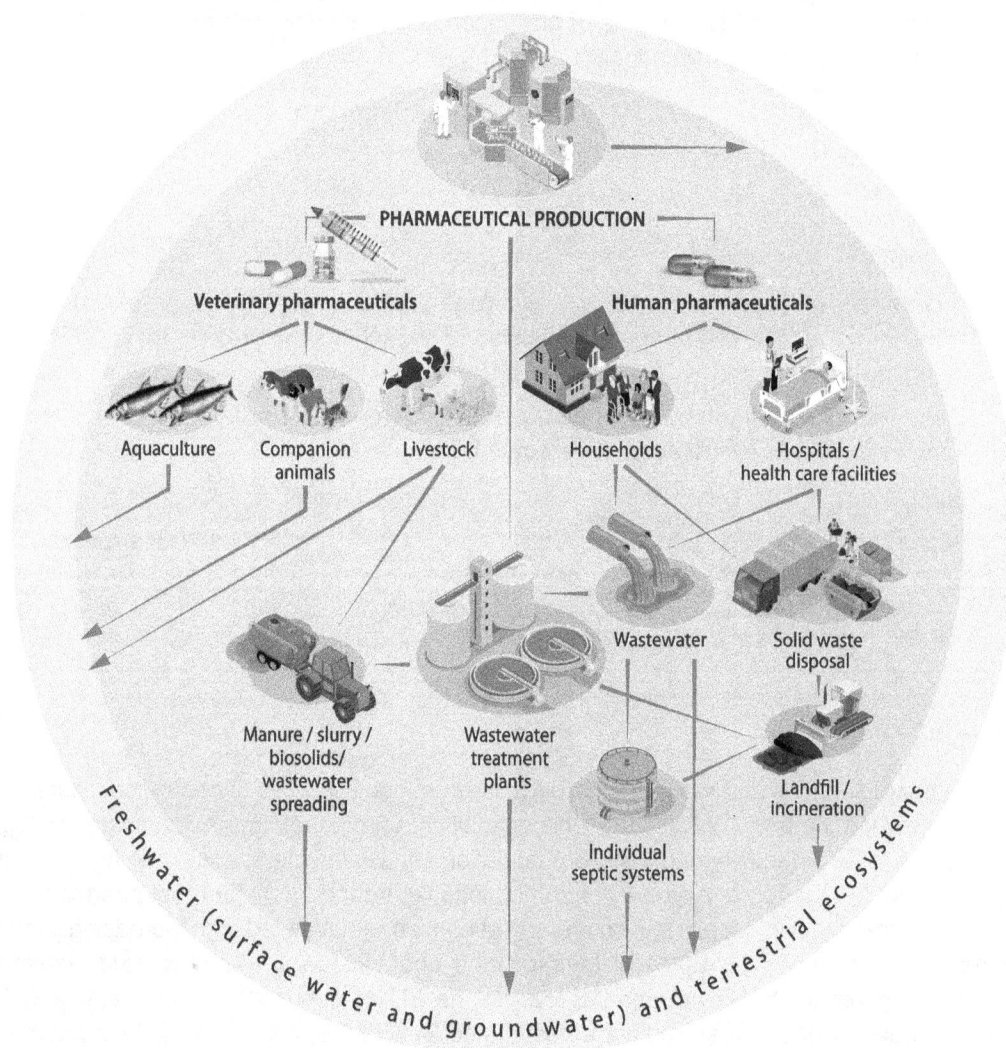

Source: (OECD, 2019[3]).

2.2. Entry pathways

The key entry pathways into freshwater and terrestrial ecosystems are the following.

2.2.1. Wastewater treatment plants (WWTP)

Conventional WWTPs are not designed to remove all pharmaceuticals, resulting in emissions into waterbodies or land in unchanged or metabolised form, if refined water is reused for agriculture (Box 2.2) (Behera et al., 2011[22]; Hollender et al., 2009[23]; Melvin and Leusch, 2016[24]; OECD, 2019[3]).

Box 2.2. End-of-pipe treatment for removal of pharmaceuticals and its limitations

The degree of pharmaceutical removal in WWTP highly varies depending on the physico-chemical properties of the APIs and the treatment process. Advanced wastewater treatment processes, such as adsorption (powered or granular) via activated carbon, ozonation, filtration by nanofiltration or reverse osmosis membranes, have been demonstrated to effectively remove most pharmaceuticals. These can achieve higher removal rates for pharmaceuticals in comparison to conventional secondary wastewater treatment (activated sludge processes, or other forms of biological treatment such as biofiltration).

However, advanced treatment technologies are generally more cost-intensive than traditional technologies and increase treatment costs by a factor of two to four, depending on technology and WWTP size (Bui et al., 2016[25]). Consequently, these technologies are not so commonly used for public WWTPs, though some countries have decided to upgrade some of their facilities. For instance, Switzerland implemented advanced wastewater treatment on a large scale using ozonation and granulated activated carbon technologies.

Decentralised point-source effluent management from hospitals, healthcare facilities, elderly homes and pharmaceutical manufacturing sites may be another route for end-of-pipe treatment. The high concentration of medicines, contrast media, cytostatics, antimicrobial resistant bacteria and pathogens[3] in hospital discharges may provide a case for emission capture and treatment at source. Currently, legislation rarely holds hospitals accountable for non-clinical wastewater discharges and excreted pharmaceuticals. Nonetheless, several newly built hospitals, for instance in the Netherlands, installed on-site treatment facilities on voluntary basis (Dutch Waste Sector, 2018[26]). Trials and pilot projects are also underway in Germany, Ireland and Switzerland (EurEau, 2019[27]).

Waste streams from pharmaceutical production facilities form another possible point-source of API emissions.[4] In most OECD countries, this source is under regulatory scrutiny and proper end-of-pipe treatment facilities are in place. However, in less developed countries, where appropriate regulatory frameworks are less defined or insufficiently enforced, this may pose a serious source of contamination that requires policy attention.

Some pharmaceuticals contained in wastewater are likely to be filtered out by WWTPs and collected in the sewage sludge. Where sewage sludge is applied on land for agricultural use ("landspreading") or used in compost, pharmaceutical residues may still enter environmental systems. Landspreading and composting are common practice in most OECD countries (Figure 2.2).

Figure 2.2. Method of sewage sludge disposal in selected OECD countries

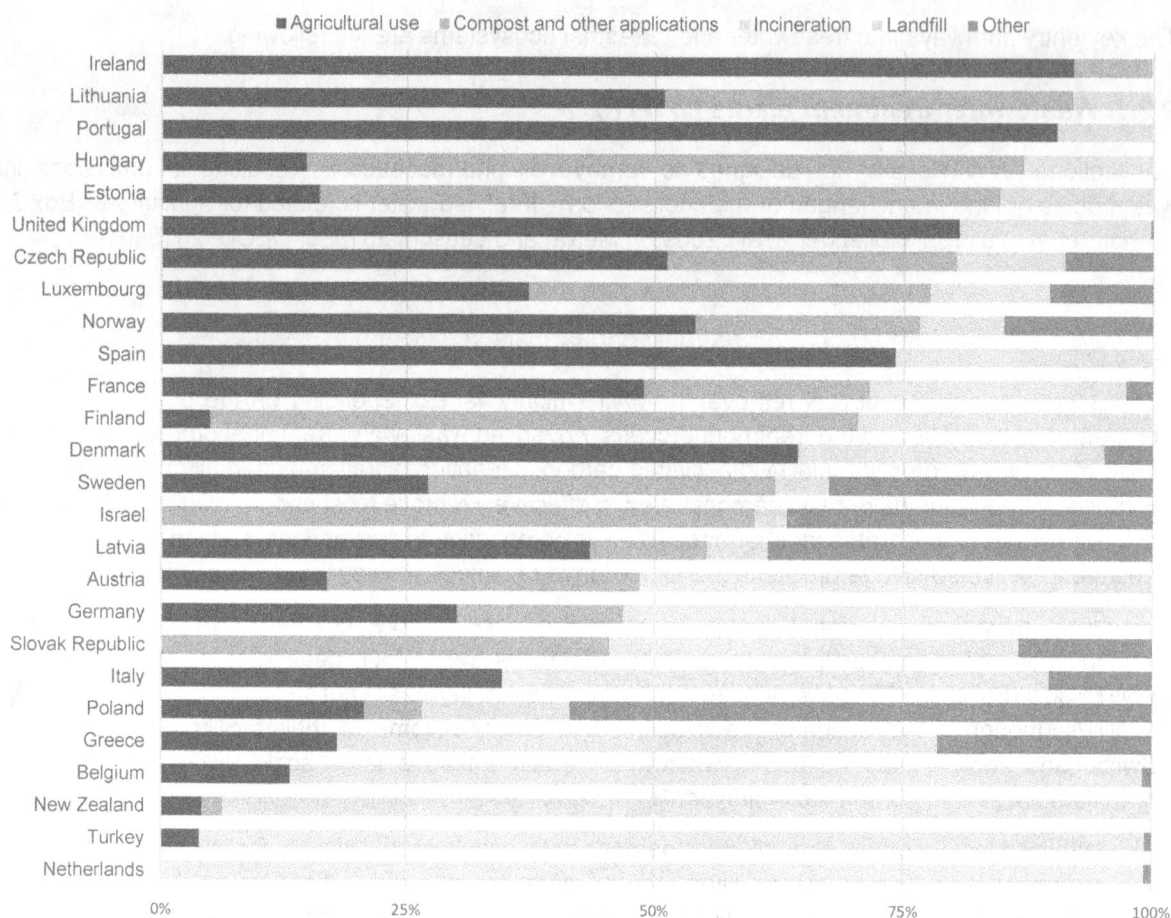

Note: "Other" category for Latvia contains biogas production and temporary storage for future use.
Source: Eurostat (2019 or nearest year) and (OECD, 2019[28]).

Combined sewer systems that collect rainwater runoff, domestic sewage and industrial wastewater in the same pipe pose a particular threat. These systems are designed to overflow occasionally and discharge excess wastewater directly into nearby streams or other water bodies. In the event of strong rainfall, combined sewer overflows lead to direct discharge of untreated human and industrial wastewater in water bodies. Additionally, in areas where households are not connected to a sewage system, pharmaceutical residues can enter the environment through discharge of wastewater from septic tanks.

2.2.2. Landfilled municipal solid waste

In OECD countries, landfill rates vary from around 90% in some countries to close to 0% in others (Figure 2.3). In occasions where mixed MSW is landfilled, pharmaceutical residues risk leaching into environmental systems if leachate is not collected and treated properly. Several studies found residues of pharmaceuticals and their metabolites in landfill leachate across the United States (Masoner et al., 2014[18]; Masoner et al., 2015[29]; Clarke et al., 2015[30]), Shanghai (Sui et al., 2017[31]) and Taiwan (Lu et al., 2016[32]). Collected landfill leachate is commonly discharged to WWTPs for treatment, where it was also proven to contribute to the loading of wastewater influents (Masoner et al., 2020[33]).

Proper management of landfill leachate is critical to avoid dispersion of pharmaceutical residues. Globally, dumpsites without proper infrastructure to manage leachate remain an important mode of MSW final disposal. Clearly, such practices create a significant risk of pharmaceutical residues entering environmental systems (World Bank, 2018[34]).

Figure 2.3. Municipal waste fate in OECD countries

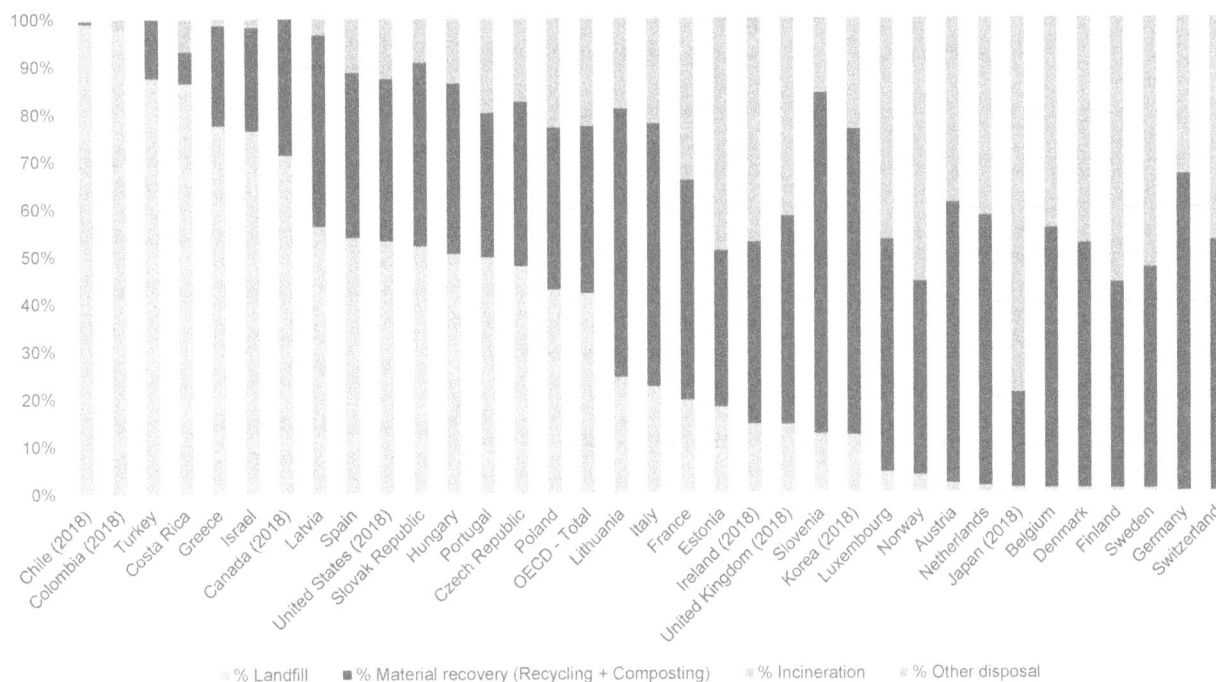

Note: Data for 2019 or nearest year.
Source: OECD Statistics.

2.3. Effects of pharmaceuticals in the environment

The vast majority of pharmaceuticals have not yet been evaluated for their long-term toxicity, occurrence or fate in the environment. Nevertheless, certain pharmaceuticals have been proven to cause undesired adverse effects on ecosystems, including increased mortality in aquatic species and changes to physiology, behaviour or reproduction[5] (Table 2.1). For example, antidepressants have been shown to alter fish behaviour; and contraceptive endocrine disrupting pharmaceuticals can interfere with fish reproduction (BIO Intelligence Service, 2013[7]; Santos et al., 2010[35]; Nash et al., 2004[6]). The German Environment Agency (UBA) estimates that 10% of the pharmaceutical products pose a potential environmental risk. Of greatest concern are hormones, antibiotics, analgesics, antidepressants and anticancer pharmaceuticals used for human health. Similar concerns apply for hormones, antibiotics and parasiticides used for veterinary pharmaceuticals (Küster and Adler, 2014[36]). The overuse and discharge of antibiotics to water bodies can also lead to mutations in animals and the development of antimicrobial resistant bacteria, posing severe risks to global health, livelihoods and food security.

Table 2.1. Examples of measured effects of certain pharmaceutical residues on aquatic organisms in laboratory studies

Therapeutic group	Examples of pharmaceutical	Impact and effected organisms	Examples of studies
Analgesics	Diclofenac, Ibuprofen	Organ damage, reduced hatching success (fish) Genotoxicity, neurotoxicity and oxidative stress (mollusc) Disruption with hormones (frog)	(Näslund et al., 2017[37]) (Mathias et al., 2018[38]) (Xia, Zheng and Zhou, 2017[39]) (Mezzelani et al., 2016[40]) (Efosa et al., 2017[41])
Antibiotics	-	Reduced growth (environmental bacteria, algae and aquatic plants)	(Roose-Amsaleg and Laverman, 2016[42]) (Guo, Boxall and Selby, 2015[43]) (Brain et al., 2008[44])
Anti-cancer	Cyclophosphamide[1], mitomycin C, fluorouracil, cisplatin, doxorubicin	Ecotoxicity, genotoxicity	(Česen et al., 2016[45]) (Zounková et al., 2007[46]) (Araújo et al., 2019[47]) (EC, 2016[48])
Antidiabetics	Metformin	Potential endocrine-disrupting effects (fish)	(Niemuth et al., 2015[49]; Crago et al., 2016[50])[2]
Anti-convulsants	Carbamazepine, phenytoin, valproic acid	Reproduction toxicity (invertebrates), development delay (fish)	(Martinez et al., 2018[51]; Ferrari et al., 2003[52])
Antifungals	Ketoconazole, clotrimazole triclosan	Reduced growth (algae, fish), reduced algae community growth, disruption of hormones (rats)	(Vestel et al., 2016[53]) (Porsbring et al., 2009[54]) (Stoker, Gibson and Zorrilla, 2010[55])
Antihistamines	Hydroxyzine, fexofenadine, diphenhydramine	Behaviour changes, growth and feeding rate (fish) Behaviour changes and reproduction toxicity (invertebrates)	(Berninger et al., 2011[56]) (Kristofco et al., 2016[57]) (Jonsson et al., 2014[58]; Meinertz et al., 2010[59])
Antiparasitics	Ivermectin	Growth and reduced reproduction (invertebrates)	(Garric et al., 2007[60])
Beta blockers	Propranolol	Reproduction behaviour (fish), reproduction toxicity (invertebrates)	(Giltrow et al., 2009[61]) (de Oliveira et al., 2016[62])
Endocrine active pharmaceuticals	E2, EE2, levonorgestrel	Disruption with hormones causing reproduction toxicity (fish, frogs)	(Kidd et al., 2007[63]) (Kvarnryd et al., 2011[64]) (Gyllenhammar et al., 2009[65]) (Armstrong et al., 2016[66]) (Moore et al., 2016[67]) (Nelles, Hu and Prins, 2011[68])
Psychiatric dugs	Fluoxetine, sertraline, oxazepam, citalopram, chlorpromazine	Behaviour changes - feeding, boldness, activity, sociality (fish) Disruption with hormones (fish) Behaviour changes - swimming and cryptic (invertebrates) Reproduction toxicity and disruption with hormones (invertebrates)	(Brodin et al., 2014[69]; Brodin et al., 2013[5]) (Kellner et al., 2016[70]) (Schultz et al., 2011[71]) (De Castro-Català et al., 2017[72]) (Di Poi et al., 2014[73]) (Campos et al., 2016[74]) (Lazzara et al., 2012[75])

Note: 1) Transformation of Cyclophosphamide and Ifosfamide. 2) NB, Caldwell et al. (2019[76]) conclude the opposite; that metformin and its transformation product guanylurea indicate no significant environmental risk.
Source: Adapted from (OECD, 2019[3]).

3 Household disposal and collection of unused pharmaceuticals

Improper household disposal of unused or expired medicine can contribute to pharmaceutical leakage into the environment. This chapter reviews the estimated amounts and disposal practices of unused or expired medicine in OECD countries.

3.1. Amount of pharmaceutical waste

The amount of medicine waste generated is affected by prescription and consumption practices. Demographic, epidemiological and lifestyle changes such as an ageing and growing population, the rise of chronic health conditions and the availability of inexpensive generic treatments and changes in clinical practice have been key drivers for increased pharmaceutical prescription and usage in OECD countries (OECD, 2021[1]).

The increase in the consumption of pharmaceuticals likely also increased the amount of UEM. Between 2000 and 2019, consumption of anti-hypertensive drugs in OECD countries increased by 65%, lipid-modifying agents increased by a factor of nearly four and the use of anti-diabetic as well as anti-depressant drugs doubled (OECD, 2021[1]).

Pharmaceutical consumption per capita strongly varies between OECD countries. Expenditure data can provide a rough proxy for the amount of drugs in circulation and the amount of medicine waste that may be generated. In 2019, spending for retail pharmaceuticals averaged USD 571 per person across OECD countries, adjusted for differences in purchasing power. Cross-country differences are marked, with spending more than double the average in the United States, followed by Germany and Canada and lowest in Mexico and Costa Rica (Figure 3.1).

Figure 3.1. Expenditure on retail pharmaceuticals per capita, 2019 (or nearest year)

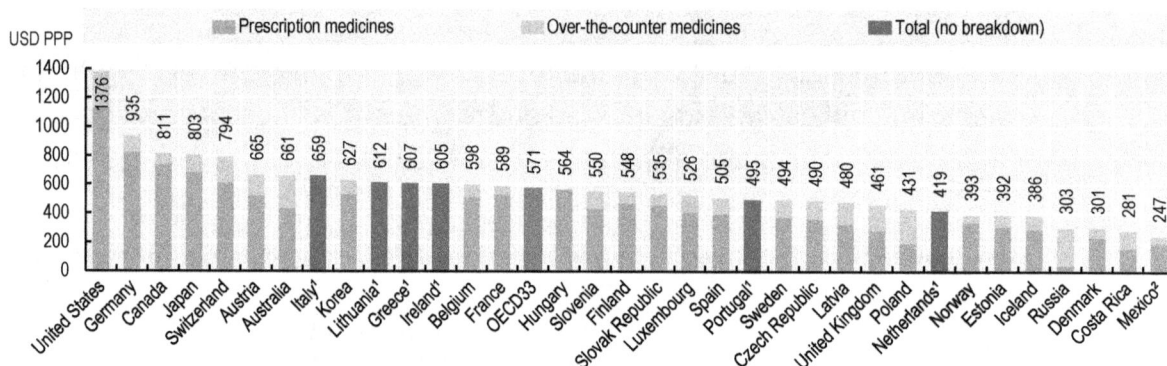

Note: 1) Includes non-durable medical goods (e.g. first aid kits and hypodermic syringes), resulting in an overestimation of around 5-10%. 2) Only includes private expenditure.
Source: OECD Health Statistics 2021.

There are many reasons why drugs can become waste:

- *No-effect, adverse reactions and/or therapy change*: Prescribed drugs prove to be unsuitable for treatment and are consequently abandoned, or the treatment is changed.
- *Non-adherence*: Patients have a poor record in taking their medication.
- *Recovery or deceased*: Patients recover more rapidly than foreseen or decease.
- *Stockpiling and/or expiring*: Patients may stock pharmaceuticals for 'just-in-case', which leads to medicines reaching their expiry date before being completely utilised (in particular over-the-counter pharmaceuticals and non-prescription drugs). Stockpiling and potential expiry is not only an issue in households but also in public buildings, hotels, marine vessels, societal institutions, prison systems and military bases where drugs are commonly stored in case of emergencies but only used infrequently (Ruhoy and Daughton, 2008[77]).
- *Prescription or purchasing error*: Patients may be prescribed or may purchase the wrong pharmaceuticals. Over prescribing can also lead to medicine waste.

Estimates of the share of medication becoming waste vary from 3% to as high as 50%. According to the European Federation of Pharmaceutical Industries and Associations (EFPIA), 3-8% of the medicinal products sold remain unused.[6] In Finland, it has been estimated that 3-4% of medicines sold go unused (by medicine price) (Finnish Pharmacy Association, 2016[78]). Law et al. (2015[13]) assume that 42% of dispensed medicines remain unused. In another US survey, six out of ten patients that got opioid painkillers prescribed, report having leftover pills at home (Kennedy-Hendricks et al., 2016[79]). Bound and Voulvoulis (2005[80]) assume 50% wastage for the United Kingdom and Musson and Townsend (2009[81]) estimate that 11% of prescribed medicines become waste.

The volume of UEM generated is difficult to trace, but a study commissioned by the French PRO Cyclamed estimated that households in France disposed of 17 600 tonnes of UEM or 259 g per capita in 2018 (2019[82]). Overall, UEM amounts up to about 0.05% of overall household waste in France (Eurostat, 2020[83]). Musson and Townsend (2009[81]) measured a concentration of 8.1 mg APIs per kg of MSW in Orange County, Florida, which they considered the lower bound of possible pharmaceutical contamination in MSW.

3.2. Household disposal practices and collection rates among OECD countries

Household disposal practices vary among (OECD) countries, critical drivers being the availability of drug take-back systems and the public awareness of these systems. Whilst a share of UEM is returned to pharmacies and collection points, disposing of UEM in solid waste bins or down household drains remains common practice in most OECD countries. In some OECD countries, where most MSW is incinerated in state-of-the-art facilities, disposal via solid household waste is one of the recommended disposal routes (e.g. Germany). Disposal via the toilets and sinks, is commonly advised against.

Figure 3.2. Household disposal practices of unused or expired medicine in selected OECD countries

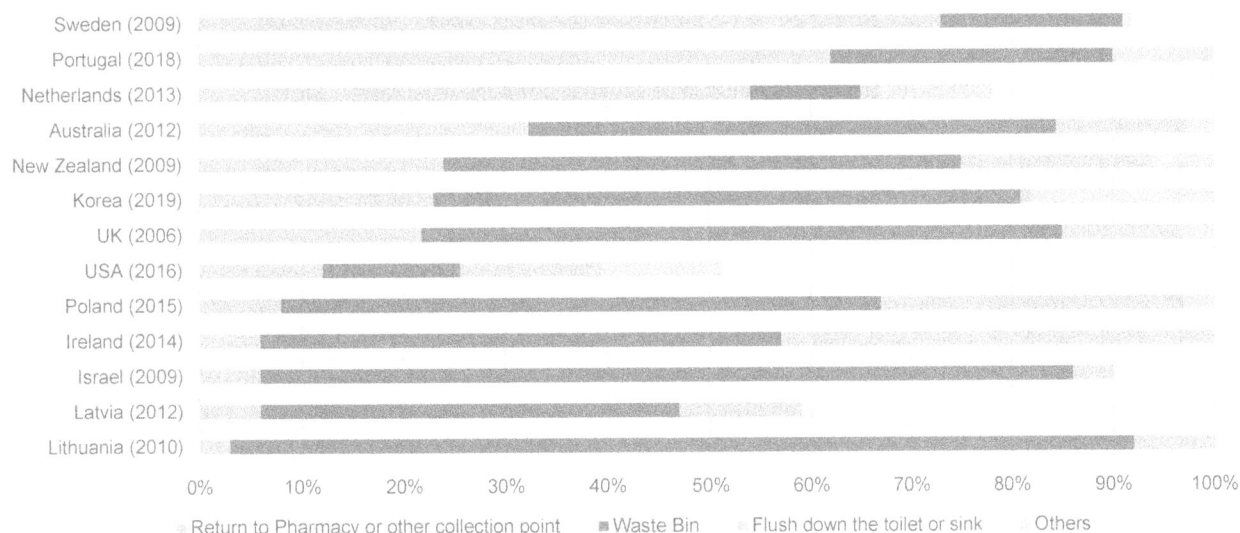

Note: Year of study indicated in brackets. Some surveys included responses of storage for later use. These were excluded in this graph, which leaves some entries <100%. "Others" includes inter alia household burning or handing to other users.
Source: Australia (Amanda J. Wheeler, Fiona Kelly, Jean Spinks, 2016[84]); Ireland (Vellinga et al., 2014[85]); Israel (Barnett-Itzhaki et al., 2016[86]); Latvia (Methonen et al., 2020[87]); Korea (DSI, 2019[88]); Lithuania (Kruopienė and Dvarionienė, 2010[89]); The Netherlands (Reitsma et al., 2013[90]); New Zealand (Braund, Peake and Shieffelbien, 2009[91]); Poland (Methonen et al., 2020[87]); Portugal (Winning Scientific Management, 2018[92]); Sweden (Persson, Sabelström and Gunnarsson, 2009[93]); UK (Bound and Voulvoulis, 2005[80]); USA (Kennedy-Hendricks et al., 2016[79]).

Sweden, Portugal and the Netherlands seem to achieve the highest shares of respondents stating to return UEM to pharmacies or collection points (more than 50%). In addition, Cyclamed (2019[82]) estimates that 62% of all UEM are returned to pharmacies in France. In Lithuania, Israel and United Kingdom most participants stated to dispose UEM in household waste bins (Figure 3.2). Alnahas et al. (2020[94]) provide a comprehensive review of the literature on household disposal practices of unused medication, where additional results can be found for non-OECD countries.

Disposal practices differ depending on the type of medicine. Liquids tend to be more often discharged in sinks or toilets, whereas solids (e.g. tablets and capsules) and semi-solid pharmaceuticals (e.g. creams and ointments) tend to be more often disposed of in solid household waste (Figure 3.3). Additionally, medicines considered to be more harmful, such as antibiotics, were more often returned to a pharmacy than over-the-counter products (e.g. cough medicine) (Tong, Peake and Braund, 2011[95]; Braund, Peake and Shieffelbien, 2009[91]; Paut Kusturica, Tomas and Sabo, 2016[96]).

Figure 3.3. Household disposal practices according to medicine type: the case of New Zealand and Germany

Question: How do you dispose of your unused 1) Liquid medications 2) Tablets/capsules 3) Ointments/creams? (n=452)

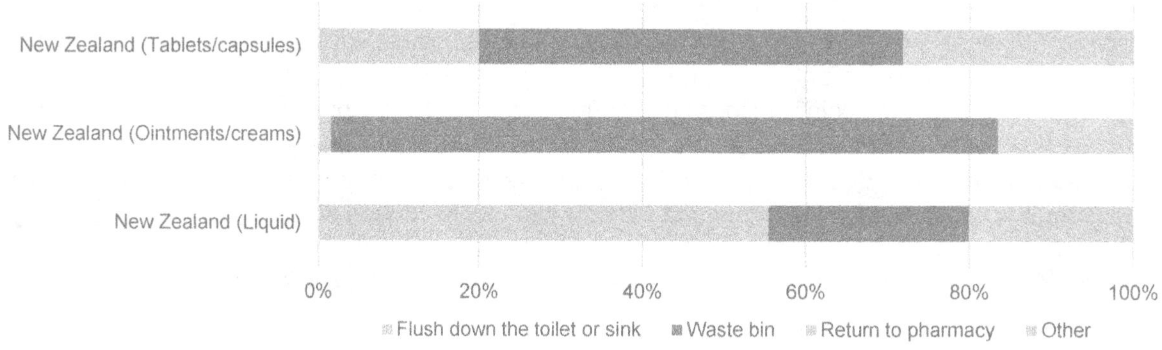

Question: Do you flush medicine leftovers (unused or expired) down the toilet? (n=1 306)

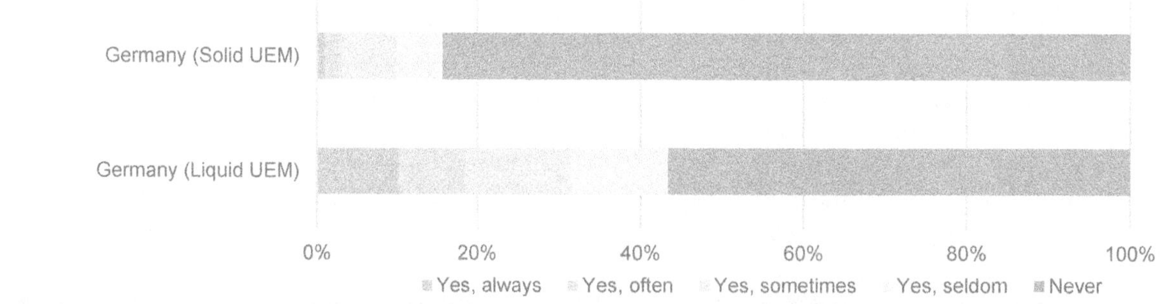

Source: (Braund, Peake and Shieffelbien, 2009[91]; Götz and Keil, 2007[97]).

In some OECD countries, home backyard burning of UEM together with other household waste also remains occasional practice in rural areas. For instance, in a survey of Lithuanian countryside households, 50% of the respondents reported burning medication (Paut Kusturica, Tomas and Sabo, 2016[96]). Whilst this practice can be considered rare in OECD countries, it may be more common in rural areas in emerging economies. Leakage into the environment via household solid waste or the drainage are also likely to be higher in countries with less developed waste management systems, especially if collected waste is destined for uncontrolled dumpsites or households.

4 Measures for minimising impacts of unused pharmaceuticals

Various measures can be taken along the lifecycle to reduce the amount and impact of unused or expired medicine. This chapter discusses measures for waste prevention, effective collection and safe final disposal, as well as the role of awareness campaigns.

Various measures can be taken along the lifecycle to minimise impacts of unused or expired pharmaceuticals. Table 4.1 depicts a number of policy interventions to reduce leakage, including waste prevention, collection and safe final disposal of waste, as well as end-of-pipe wastewater treatment.

Table 4.1. Measures for minimising impact of unused or expired pharmaceuticals

	Measure	Description
Waste prevention	Disease prevention	Emission prevention through disease prevention.
	Personalised and precision medicine	Medication that is better targeted to patients' needs can result in fewer and more effective treatments.
	Dimensioning	Reducing packaging sizes (particularly for new drug treatments and starter packs) reduces risk of accumulation of unused or expired drugs in households.
	Marketplace for unused pharmaceuticals	A marketplace for unused close-to-expiry-date (unopened) medicines provides better matching of supply and demand.
Collection and safe final disposal of waste	Collection in mixed municipal solid waste and controlled final disposal	Collection in mixed MSW and incineration in state-of-the-art incinerators.
	Separate collection: Drug take-back schemes	Take-back schemes prevent uncontrolled and improper household disposal of unused or expired drugs.
	Extended producer responsibility schemes	EPR puts the responsibility of the collection and end-of-life treatment of pharmaceuticals on the producer.
	Education campaigns	Education and information campaigns inform about optimal household disposal routes.
End-of-pipe treatment	Upgrade wastewater treatment plants	Upgrade wastewater treatment plants to capture emissions of excreted and discarded drugs in sewage.

4.1. Avoidance of pharmaceutical waste

Bekker et al. (2018[98]) estimate that approximately 40% of UEM generated in the Netherlands can be prevented.[7] Improved disease prevention, personalised medication, precision medicine and improved dimensioning of packaging sizes all reduce the risk of accumulation and improper disposal of unused drugs in households. Each of these approaches, as well as possible policy measures, are discussed more extensively in the 2019 OECD report on *Pharmaceutical Residues in Freshwater* (OECD, 2019[3]).

Marketplaces for unused close-to-expiry-date medicines provide better matching of supply and demand and can thus prevent pharmaceutical wastage. Similarly, redistribution of unused medicines can avoid waste and can lead to significant economic savings. Bekker et al. (2018[98]) estimate that approximately 19% of UEM returned in the Netherlands would be eligible for re-dispensing.[8]

In most OECD countries, resale or re-dispensing of unused medicines is currently not practiced due to concerns regarding counterfeits, quality assurance and consequent legal restraints, but a number of initiatives exist (Box 4.1).

> **Box 4.1. Examples of marketplaces of unused or close-to-expiry-date medicines in OECD countries**
>
> PharmaSwap in the Netherlands allows certified pharmacists to sell unused/undamaged medicines before they expire to other pharmacies who are in demand, often at reduced prices. The platform currently connects eight hospital pharmacies, 551 community pharmacies and eight wholesalers. Since its launch, it redistributed more than 3 500 packages and avoided procurement costs of more than EUR 600 000 by making more efficient use of pharmaceutical stocks (PharmaSwap, 2022[99]).
>
> Sirum and Prescription Promise are two US start-ups that aim to collect and redistribute unused drugs to low-income patients and people in need. Donating patients and pharmacies can send in their unused medicines. Others can apply for these drugs by submitting a prescription form (Prescription Promise, 2020[100]; Sirum, 2020[101]). Similarly, the catholic social service organisation Caritas in Italy holds periodic collection events to collect unused medicines for redistribution to people in need.
>
> In the Netherlands, a government-funded study is currently assessing the feasibility of implementing a re-dispensing process for unused novel oral anticancer agents. The study will redistribute medication that remains unused by oncology patients, and a first pilot includes 1 150 patients from four hospitals (ZonMw, 2020[102]).

4.2. Collection schemes and take-back systems for household pharmaceutical waste

Separate collection systems help avoid environmental leakage caused by flushing UEM in the drainage or by mixing UEM with solid household waste that is destined for landfill without leachate collection (Masoner et al., 2014[18]).

A variety of different collection schemes, take-back systems and stewardship programs are in place in OECD countries that aim to recover and manage waste pharmaceuticals. These can differ in many ways, including the scope of medicine waste covered, financing, collection routes, legislation and recovery efficacies. On-site receptacles at pharmacies constitute the most common collection system. One-day collection events or mail-back envelopes are also offered in some countries (e.g. United States). Some programs rely only on government funding (e.g. Australia) while others are financed by contributions from the pharmaceutical industry or from pharmacies that provide support on a voluntary basis or driven by extended producer responsibility (EPR) legislation.

Notably, not all OECD countries have implemented separate collection schemes for UEM, either because medicine disposal in households via mixed solid household waste is considered more cost-efficient (and still environmentally sound) (Box 4.2), or because the collection system is not mature enough to cope with additional small volume streams (see Annex A for a list of different collection schemes and approaches in OECD countries).

> **Box 4.2. Separate collection schemes – a necessity for environmentally sound management of medicine waste?**
>
> The environmental necessity of separate collection of pharmaceutical waste depends largely on the fate of mixed municipal waste (Figure 2.3). In countries where all mixed household waste is either destined for incineration in facilities with proper air cleaning and ash treatment, or in sanitary landfills with performant capture and treatment of the leachate, the risk for entry of active pharmaceutical ingredients (API) in the environment is limited.
>
> Nevertheless, even in mature waste management systems, throwing UEM in mixed household waste could raise health concerns related to the risk of abuse by third parties accessing household bins. The US Drug Enforcement Agency recommends to households in cases when no take-back programme is available to mix medicines with undesirable substances, such as used coffee grounds or cat litter before disposal in solid household waste to avoid misuse (DEA, 2020[103]).
>
> The evaluation of environmental and health risks differs from country to country. Countries that deem the risks sufficiently important typically introduce a separate collection scheme for unused medicine. Other countries have decided that the limited environmental and health risks do not justify collecting UEM separately. The overview in Annex A highlights the divergence of national policies.
>
> In Europe, the EU List of Waste (2000/532/EC) only categorises cytotoxic and cytostatic medicines as hazardous. Other unused medicines are not categorised as hazardous. The EU Directive 2004/27/EC, Article 127b requires EU Member States to "ensure that appropriate collection systems are in place for medicinal products that are unused or have expired." (European Commission, 2004[104]). It is left to individual member states to determine whether separate collection through take back systems is necessary to ensure appropriate disposal. Most EU countries have opted for separate collection, but others such as Germany do not have a separate collection scheme at national level (Methonen et al., 2020[87]).
>
> In **Germany** drug return schemes are only in place in some local areas. At the national level, it is recommended to dispose of pharmaceuticals in solid household waste, as all MSW is only landfilled after prior thermal treatment (NaWaM, 2020[105]). This approach is accompanied with information and awareness campaigns, informing citizens of safe household disposal routes in each region and discouraging the flushing of UEM (UBA, 2018[106]).

If separately collected, final disposal of UEM is ideally done by high temperature incineration (of at least 1 000°C), equipped with adequate flue gas cleaning, to ensure destruction or removal of the substances of concern (Methonen et al., 2020[87]; EU JRC, 2019[107]). However, some countries, where municipal solid waste incineration is pervasive and households are instructed to dispose of UEM through mixed household waste, consider that incineration at lower temperatures (typically 850°C or higher) is also safe. The EU Waste Codes only classify two classes of medicines as hazardous wastes, cytostatic and cytotoxic medicines (EWC code: 18 01 08) (European Commission, 2000[108]). However, some EU countries go beyond the European classification (e.g. Finland and Denmark classify all UEM as hazardous) and consequently require high temperature incineration for a larger share of UEM (Methonen et al., 2020[87]).

4.2.1. Voluntary collection schemes

In some countries, such as the Netherlands, drug take-back schemes are implemented in the form of voluntary approaches. Pharmacies and the pharmaceutical industry implement these systems driven by their corporate social responsibility commitments. Other motivating factors are pressure from consumers or pre-empting regulatory requirements (Box 4.3).

Box 4.3. Selected examples of voluntary drug take-back schemes

In the **Netherlands,** pharmacies are not legally obliged to take back leftover medicines from citizens. However, many pharmacies voluntarily act as a collection centre on behalf of the municipalities. Once collected, municipalities generally pick up the waste at the pharmacies and take care of its safe disposal (KNMP, 2020[109]). Surveys indicate that a majority of the population (54%) use the return scheme and dispose of unused medication via this channel (Reitsma et al., 2013[90]).

Similarly, in **Finland** pharmacies act as voluntary collection points. Municipalities provide waste collection bins to pharmacies and organise further treatment. It is estimated that 60-80% of unused medicines are returned to pharmacies by Finnish citizens (Methonen et al., 2020[87]).

In **Poland**, some municipal offices, health care centres or pharmacies voluntarily collect and dispose of UEM in special disposal containers financed by local governments. But the availability of collection points appears to be sparse, especially in smaller towns and rural areas (Rogowska et al., 2019[110]).

4.2.2. Government-funded collection schemes

In other countries, such as Australia, pharmaceutical waste collection is funded and organised by national or local governments (Box 4.4).

Box 4.4. Selected examples of government-funded drug take-back schemes

In **Australia**, the National Return of Unwanted Medicines Scheme (NatRUM), established in 1999, is a national program that collects unwanted medicine via pharmacies. While the pharmaceutical industry is aware and supportive of the RUM project, the program is entirely financed by the Australian Health Department. Collection rates have steadily increased and are now at around 60 tonnes per month (32 g/capita per year) (NatRUM, 2020[111]). However, awareness and use of the scheme are still limited; only 18% of respondents had heard of the NatRUM Project and the most common form of medicine disposal reported by Australian consumers continues to be the household bin followed by toilets or drains (Bettington et al., 2018[112]; Kelly et al., 2018[113]).

In **Switzerland**, pharmaceutical waste is classified as hazardous waste and should not be disposed of in normal household bins. UEM from households can be returned to the pharmacies or to designated disposal points. The funding of these schemes differs per Canton. In some Cantons the scheme is government-funded while in other Cantons pharmacies bear the cost, which can be passed on to the consumer.

4.2.3. Extended producer responsibility (EPR) schemes for pharmaceutical waste

Several countries and provinces, such as France, Spain and Portugal have pursued an EPR approach to managing household medication (Box 4.5). By obliging pharmaceutical companies to collect and destroy unwanted pharmaceuticals that they have put on the market, EPR shifts the economic and organisational burden of unused drugs collection and disposal from the government to the pharmaceutical industry. As a result, EPR implements the "producer pays principle", moving waste management costs from taxpayers to producers. Companies can internalise these costs in the price and can, in theory, provide services more cost-efficiently.

EPR systems in pharmaceutical waste streams are commonly organised as collective producer responsibility schemes (CPRs), where producers pay a contribution to a producer responsibility organisation (PRO), which manages the collection and safe disposal of UEM (Figure 4.1).

Figure 4.1. Physical and financial flows for Collective Producer Responsibility (CPR) schemes

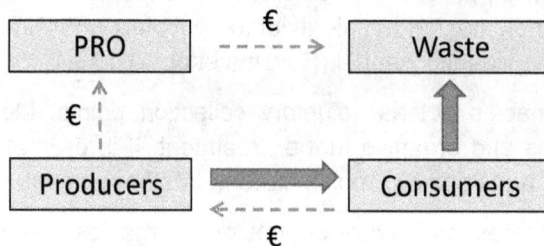

Source: (OECD, 2016[114]).

Box 4.5. Selected examples of national and subnational EPR schemes for pharmaceutical waste

In France, pharmacies are obliged to collect unused medicinal products free of charge since 2007 (Legifrance, 2007[115]). Since 2009, pharmaceuticals are included in the national framework for EPR. Pharmaceutical companies finance the collection and disposal of unused drugs from households and pharmacies act as collection points. The ministry of environment gives a six-year accreditation to a PRO that organises the scheme. This mandate currently lies with Cyclamed (2022-27) (Legifrance, 2021[116]). Because of the mandatory participation, the program has a 100% subscription rate for pharmacies (22 000 pharmacies), pharmaceutical companies (191 companies) and pharmaceutical wholesalers (195 agencies). According to Cyclamed, 78% of all patients participate in the scheme and return unused medicines to collection points. In 2018, 10 827 (161 g/capita) tonnes of unused pharmaceuticals were collected and sent for incineration with energy recovery (Cyclamed, 2019[82]). The total cost of the collection scheme amounts to EUR 10 million and is financed by a contribution of producers of EUR 0.0032 per medication pack excluding VAT. The amount of unused drugs accumulating in French households has steadily decreased, from 878 g per capita in 2010 to 614 g per capita in 2018 (CSA, 2018[117]).

Sweden has a long tradition (since 1971) of returning unused pharmaceuticals to pharmacies. Originally, drug-return schemes were introduced by the Swedish monopoly pharmacy chain (Apoteket AB) for health security reasons. In 2009, Sweden introduced an EPR scheme for pharmaceuticals (SFS 2009:1031) including provisions for the take-back of left-over household pharmaceuticals.[9] Unlike many other countries, the responsibility for financing and organising collection and safe disposal of UEM lies entirely with the pharmacies. The scheme is supposed to be financed by trade margins, though in some cases these are insufficient, and pharmacies carry the remaining costs.[10] The scheme functions well and has achieved a high public awareness. In 2020, the total amount of medicines collected amounted to 1 400 tonnes (136 g/capita) (Swedish Pharmacy Association, 2021[118]).

In **Canada**, pharmaceutical waste management is organised at the provincial level. The first provincial EPR scheme was established in British Columbia in 1997 and similar programs have been developed in Manitoba (2011), Ontario (2012) and on Prince Edward Island (2015) (Government Manitoba, 2010[119]; Government Ontario, 2014[120]; Prince Edward Island Government, 2015[121]; British Columbia, 2017[122]). In the Canadian EPR systems, producers can either set up their own return program or sign up with a PRO. In Canada, the Health Products Stewardship Association (HPSA) is the only PRO currently managing pharmaceutical returns on behalf of pharmaceutical producers. The association is fully funded by brand-owners and contributions are based on market share. Retail pharmacies commonly act as collection sites. The Association has currently over 148 member producers and close to 5 746 retail pharmacies registered. It collected 433 tonnes of UEM in 2019 (20 g/capita) in these provinces (HPSA, 2020[123]). In other provinces, take back is managed by voluntary programs, which are funded by pharmacies, manufacturers or government agencies. For example, Nova Scotia's Medication Disposal Program is a voluntary system run by the pharmacy association (PANS, 2019[124]). In Quebec pharmacies are obliged to take back returned UEM, but no EPR regulation is in place that secures the financing.

Similarly, the **United States** (US) does not have a national EPR drug take-back program, but an increasing number of mandatory programs (EPR) can be found at the state or local level. As of 2018, there were 25 local EPR laws in the US: 3 at state-level, 18 at county-level and 4 at city-level (New York Department of Environmental Conservation, 2018[125]). All of these are mandatory EPR programs and are funded by pharmaceutical manufacturers and run by MED-Project, the PRO, on behalf of pharmaceutical companies. The United States also has a national voluntary drug take-back program. The US Drug Enforcement Administration (DEA) organises biannual collection events, the "National Take Back Days." The last two events in April and October 2021, recovered 420 and 372 tonnes of UEM (2.4 g/capita for 2021) (DEA, 2022[126]). Additionally, following a 2010 change in US federal law,[11] DEA developed regulation allowing pharmacies to collect unwanted pharmaceuticals from households, and allowing them to utilise mail-back envelopes. Where no take-back program exists, the US Food and Drug Administration (FDA) provides guidelines on how to safely dispose drugs in household waste[12] (FDA, 2020[127]).

Table 4.2. Examples of pharmaceutical EPR systems in OECD countries

Country	PRO	Funding	Collection points	Additional information
Mexico	SINGREM	Pharmaceutical industry	Pharmacies	An online search engine exists to find the nearest collection point.
Sweden	Pharmacies	Pharmacies	Pharmacies	Pharmacies are responsible individually. A loyalty program rewards customers when medicines are returned.
Spain	SIGRE	Pharmaceutical industry	Pharmacies	An interactive online map shows the nearest collection points.
Portugal	Valormed	Pharmaceutical industry	Pharmacies	
Hungary	Recyclomed	Pharmaceutical industry	Pharmacies and notified collection centres	
France	Cyclamed	Pharmaceutical industry	Pharmacies	A mobile application allows interaction with consumers and allows them to locate the nearest collection points.
Belgium	Bonusage	Pharmaceutical industry	Pharmacies	

Note: See Annex A for a more comprehensive list of pharmaceutical waste management systems in OECD countries.

Collection rates differ among the schemes. For the countries where data was accessible, per-capita collection rates seem to be highest in France and Sweden, followed by Portugal and Spain (blue columns in Figure 4.2).

Pharmaceutical waste generation and collection rates also depend on the initial per-capita consumption. The ratio of collected waste and expenditure can be used as a rough proxy to inform about the effectiveness of different collection schemes (yellow dots in Figure 4.2).[13] Sweden and France, with around 270 mg collected per USD spent, seem to be the most effective systems in collecting UEM. Portugal and

Spain, with 200-220 mg/USD also perform relatively well. All four countries with high ratios have an EPR system in place with full and harmonised national coverage and with collection points at pharmacies. In Portugal, Spain and France, a producer responsibility organisation (PRO) collectively implements responsibilities of producers and organises the pick-up and disposal of collected waste medicines as well as the reporting, whereas in Sweden, pharmacies organise the collection individually. A share of the PRO budget is dedicated to awareness campaigns aimed at waste prevention and better patient compliance. Some countries (e.g. France) already witnessed a decrease in the collection rate due to waste prevention measures such as reduced prescriptions, precision medicine and better patient compliance.

Figure 4.2. Per capita collection rates of pharmaceutical waste in selected OECD countries [g/capita] (blue bars), compared to expenditure (yellow dots)

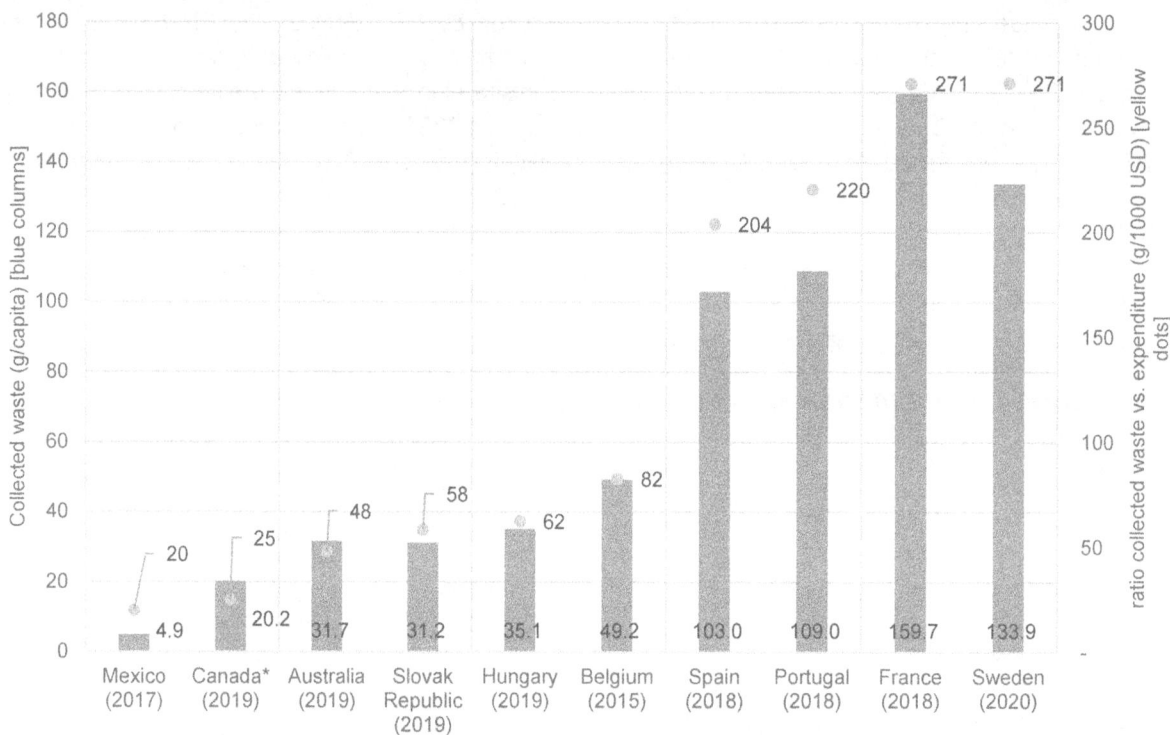

Note: *Canada includes per-capita values for BC, MB, ON and PEI only. Per capita values were calculated from collection amount (nearest date) and population data. Expenditure values are dated 2019.
Source: Australia (NatRUM, 2020[111]),Belgium (Belgian Pharmacy Association, 2016[128]), Canada (HPSA, 2020[123]), France (Cyclamed, 2019[82]), Hungary (Recyclomed, 2019[129]), Mexico (Singrem, 2018[130]), Portugal (VALORMED, 2020[131]), Slovak Republic, Spain (Survey data), Sweden (Swedish Pharmacy Association, 2021[118]), Expenditure (per capita): OECD Health Statistics 2021.

In most countries PROs are financed by contributions of pharmaceutical companies (producers) through EPR fees. The fees are charged based on market share, but methodologies and rates differ depending on national contexts. In countries where a per-package fee is charged and where this data was available, these ranged from 0.14 EUR cents per package in Hungary and 0.607 EUR cents per package in Spain. In some OECD countries additional EPR fees arise for outer packaging.

Figure 4.3. EPR fees of producer responsibility organisations in selected OECD countries

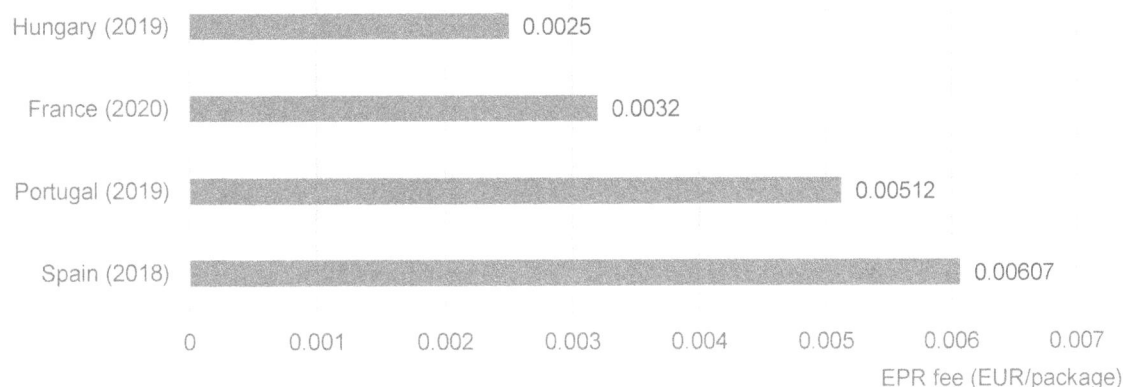

Source: Author own, based on questionnaires and interviews.

Assessing the efficiency and effectiveness of the systems in different countries is challenging due to the disparate conditions. Nonetheless, some good practices for a well-functioning pharmaceutical waste management system can be identified.

A sustainable source of *funding* is required to ensure the long-term operation of a scheme. Many countries structure funding responsibility along the "producer pays principle", in form of an EPR scheme, with financial contributions from the pharmaceutical industry. In other cases, public entities (either municipalities or national governments) cover the cost of collection and treatment.

The responsibility for *all costs should be clearly allocated*. For example, clarifying who should carry the costs related to the role of pharmacies as collection points (dedicating commercial space, administrative costs and possibly also costs of disposal of packaging) is needed.[14]

Coherence of communication and harmonisation of systems is important to achieve compliance of users (citizens) and adherents (the industry). Since some countries manage pharmaceutical waste at the sub-national or municipal level, the multitude of different schemes can lead to confusion. For instance, in Canada some provinces have EPR schemes whereas others do not. In the United States a total of 23 different schemes currently exist at the state, county or city level. In the EU single market, each country sets its own approach.

Additionally, EPR systems should foresee *mechanisms to deal with the risks of online sales of medicines*. Online sales are creating free-riding opportunities as consumers are able to buy more easily from sellers in other regions/countries that do not always respect local EPR obligations. The use of mail-order medicines and online pharmacies (ePharmacies) has increased and the global ePharmacy market is projected to more than triple between 2018 and 2026 (Business Fortune Insights, 2019[132]). If no appropriate legislation is in place, ePharmacies could avoid producer/retailer/distributor obligations (and costs), whilst adding to the waste stream, undermining the financial stability of the EPR system.[15]

4.3. Awareness campaigns

The limited awareness of consumers about proper disposal routes and drug take-back schemes weakens their impact on disposal practices in many countries (Box 4.6) (Paut Kusturica, Tomas and Sabo, 2016[96]). In a US survey, 45% of the respondents did not recall receiving information on proper disposal practices (Kennedy-Hendricks et al., 2016[79]). In Portugal, almost half of the respondents consider the current dissemination to be insufficient and would like to receive more information about existing disposal options (Winning Scientific Management, 2018[92]). In Latvia, 60% of respondents admitted to not being aware of how to dispose of UEM properly (Methonen et al., 2020[87]) and a survey conducted in the Netherlands concluded that 17.5% were unaware that liquid medicines should not be flushed (Dutch Sustainable Pharmacy Coalition, 2020[133]).

Box 4.6. Evidence of limited awareness of existing drug-return schemes in OECD countries

In **Lithuania**, awareness about the legal obligation of pharmacies to act as a collection centre for UEM, is limited and awareness campaigns are only scarcely available (Kümmerer and Hempel, 2010[21]). As a result, citizens often dispose of medicines along with their household waste (89% in towns, 50% in the countryside) or by flushing down the drain (8% of town residents). In the countryside open burning of pharmaceutical waste also remains common practice (Kruopienė and Dvarionienė, 2010[89]).

In **Israel** there is no mandatory legislation regarding the collection and disposal of household pharmaceutical waste, nor are there campaigns conducted to educate citizens about the safe disposal of pharmaceutical waste. Whilst UEM can be returned to pharmacies on a voluntary basis, only 6% of the interviewed citizens make use of this option, probably due to limited awareness (Barnett-Itzhaki et al., 2016[86]).

Information campaigns can increase the awareness and use-rate of take-back schemes (Box 4.7). When developing effective awareness campaigns the following considerations are important:

- Target group: Identify the target group to customise the design and communication channels of the campaign. Elderly (>65 years) are the age group with the highest rates of medicine prescription and possibly also the age group where most drugs accumulate and/or expire. Additionally, Cyclamed, the French PRO, identified that motivating young people is a particular challenge as they tend to have relatively few drugs stored and visit pharmacies less frequently.
- Information gap: The reasons for a lack of participation should be analysed before designing the awareness campaign. For instance, whereas solid pharmaceutical waste is more commonly returned to pharmacies, liquid drugs and creams seem to be more often disposed of via toilets and sinks (Braund, Peake and Shieffelbien, 2009[91]).

Box 4.7. Examples of awareness campaigns in OECD countries

The #Medsdisposal campaign is a European initiative jointly co-ordinated by several European supply chain and healthcare organisations. The initiative aims to combat the negative impacts of mismanaged pharmaceuticals on the environment by informing customers about disposal routes and available take back systems in different European countries. This is complemented by media campaigns in different languages (MedsDisposal, 2021[134]).

The DUMP (Disposal of Unwanted Medicines Properly) Campaign conducted in New Zealand has been considered effective in educating the general public about the safe disposal of UEM. The Project is supported by different health agencies in New Zealand (SaferX, 2017[135]).

The German education campaign: "No pharmaceuticals down the toilet or sink!" is also considered a cost-efficient and effective information campaign (UBA, 2018[106]).

Other approaches can also lead to increased awareness and behavioural change. For example: special instructions for disposal that appear on the outer packaging of medicinal products or in the information leaflet; nudges such as 'challenges' or 'saving accounts' to return medication to pharmacies; and product ecolabelling to inform consumer choices (Table 4.3).

Doctors and pharmacists have a key role in prescribing and informing the public about safe medicine disposal practices. Therefore awareness campaigns and the availability of customised tools for health professionals can improve the overall awareness of the population. For example, advanced practitioner trainings and environmental classification schemes help practitioners to prescribe medication taking into account environmental criteria. The Swedish Association of pharmaceutical industry developed such a scheme, which so far covers around 200 APIs. There is interest to extend this initiative within the EU.

Table 4.3. Possible measures to increase awareness and induce behaviour change

Measure	Description	Example initiative
Information campaigns	Information campaigns can increase the awareness and use-rate of take-back schemes. They can be financed and managed by public authorities, the private sector, NGOs or be an accompanying requirement in the design of EPR schemes.	The Medsdisposal campaign, a joint initiative between European healthcare, industry and pharmacist's associations, aims to provide information on how to dispose of UEM appropriately in different EU countries.
Incentives for returning medication to pharmacies	Incentives for returning medications to collection points, such as refunds or other rewards to nudge consumers to adopt appropriate disposal practices.	In Sweden most pharmacy chains offer bonus credit points to consumers for returning UEM to collection points.
Product information provision	Special instructions for disposal that appear on the outer packaging of medicinal products, in the patient information leaflet or on the medication label can lead to greater awareness and behaviour change of consumers.	In the EU, providing this information is mandatory.[1]
Product ecolabelling	Ecolabels on the environmental impact of different medicines and other product information systems can inform consumer choice, selection and awareness and assist doctors in decision making when prescribing medication.	In the Stockholm Region in Sweden, a 'wise list' was created, which provides medication recommendations based on scientific documentation regarding efficacy and safety, pharmaceutical effectiveness. This list is distributed to doctors and made publicly available (Janusinfro, 2022[136]).
Environmental classification schemes	Similar to product ecolabelling, environmental classification schemes allow doctors to make informed prescription choices.	The Swedish Association of pharmaceutical industry (Läkemedelsindustriföreningens Service AB) developed an environmental classification scheme, which so far covers ca. 200 APIs. Pharmaceutical companies can voluntarily enter information, which is then made accessible online for consumers and prescribers (FASS, 2020[137]).

Note: 1) The EU Directive 2004/27/EC (Article 54j) states that "reference to any appropriate collection system in place shall appear on the outer packaging of medicinal products or, where there is no outer packaging, on the immediate packaging".

5 Policy recommendations

This final chapter concludes with a set of policy recommendations on the effective management of pharmaceutical household waste.

Policies to address pharmaceutical waste should take a lifecycle approach, including source-directed, user-orientated and waste management focused measures, targeting the full range of stakeholders and using a combination of voluntary, economic and regulatory instruments.

- *Recommendation 1*: The first priority is to prevent unused or expired medicine. A number of approaches can help avoid the generation of pharmaceutical waste, such as improved disease prevention, precision medicine and improved dimensioning of packaging sizes.[16]

- *Recommendation 2*: Marketplaces and redistribution platforms for unused close-to-expiry-date medicines provide better matching of supply and demand and contribute to waste prevention and economic savings. Countries should assess possibilities for redistribution. Initiatives in the Netherlands and the United States have highlighted the potential of these measures.

- *Recommendation 3*: The collection of unused medication has to be customised to the national context and local challenges. Separate collection of UEM is useful to control the impacts on the environment and public health by:

  - Lowering the risk of abuse or accidents by third parties accessing household bins to recover UEM.

  - Reducing the risk of UEM, in particular liquids, creams and ointments, being flushed down the drain and contaminating waterways.

  - Avoiding entry of active pharmaceutical ingredients (API) into the environment, via other pathways, such as solid waste, particularly in countries, regions or municipalities where state-of-the-art household waste incineration is not widespread.

- *Recommendation 4:* If a separate collection system is deemed relevant, EPR schemes have shown to be an effective approach to organise environmentally sound collection and treatment.[17] Alternative approaches such as publicly financed take-back schemes can also be effective but do not implement the polluter pays principle.

- *Recommendation 5:* If an EPR scheme is implemented, monitoring and prosecution of freeriding by ePharmacies, online sales and postal deliveries should be set up in order to maintain a level playing field for industry and to ensure long-term financing of the scheme.[18]

- *Recommendation 6*: The following considerations can further support the design of separate collection systems:

  - Drug take-back should be available to consumers all year-round at convenient collection points and free of charge to minimise transaction costs compared to other disposal routes. Pharmacies have shown to be suitable collection points.

  - Targets and regular review periods can ensure an economically efficient functioning of producer responsibility organisations (PROs) in EPRs. For instance, the French EPR law accredits PRO mandates in a five-year cycle.

- *Recommendation 7*: The limited awareness of consumers about proper disposal routes and/or the existence of drug take-back schemes induces improper household disposal. In order to increase the awareness, governments and PROs should foresee well-focused communication campaigns. Key elements for impactful communication are:

  - Identify the target group and the optimal communication channel. Set up indicators and benchmark to monitor the effectiveness of the campaign.

  - Focus on liquid pharmaceuticals, since studies indicate that this product group is still often discarded via the sink or toilet.

  - Visible sorting instructions on the packaging contributes to the awareness about take-back facilities.[19]

  - Nudging is a strong tool for behavioural change. Programs such as 'bonus points' given by pharmacies in Sweden motivate citizens to return UEM to pharmacies.

Annex A. List of pharmaceutical waste management systems in OECD countries

Country	National drug collection programme	Legislation	Collection method	Funding	Source
Australia	State-funded national programme (NatRUM)		Collection at community pharmacies (voluntary participation)	Government (Australian Health Department)	(NatRUM, 2020[111])
Austria	Voluntary collection by pharmacies		Unused medicine should be returned to pharmacies or to public collection points	Collaborative funding by local governments and pharmacies	(Oesterreich.gv.at, 2022[138]; Stadt Wien, 2022[139])
Belgium	National EPR scheme, infrastructure and costs negotiated by region (Wallonia, Flanders, Brussels)	Mandatory legislation in place		Funded by pharmaceutical industry and wholesalers	
Canada	Four provincial EPR programs	Provincial legislation in place	Retail pharmacies commonly act as collection sites	Industry	(Vargas, 2018[140])
Chile		No legislation and drug take-back system in place. Recommendations to safely dispose in sealed package in household waste			
Czech Republic	Pharmacies are required to take back unused medicine	National legislation issued by the State Institute of Drug Control	Pharmacies	Funded by the state through regional authorities	(State Institute For Drug Control, 2007[141])
Denmark	Locally organised collection programs	Mandatory legislation in place	Pharmacies or designated municipal collection points	Local government	(Methonen et al., 2020[87])
Estonia	Mandatory take back collection systems via pharmacies and municipal collection points	Waste Act, and municipal waste handling rules	Pharmacies and hazardous waste collection points	Pharmacies finance the waste collection process, municipalities partially finance local collection	(Methonen et al., 2020[87])

MANAGEMENT OF PHARMACEUTICAL HOUSEHOLD WASTE © OECD 2022

Country	Scheme / Programme	Legislation	Collection	Financing	Source
Finland	Collection systems via pharmacies and collection points. Municipalities are responsible for collection, transportation and disposal of UEM	Pharmaceutical waste produced by households is classified as hazardous waste and must be collected separately (Waste Act)	Community pharmacies and municipal collection points	Local municipality	(Methonen et al., 2020[87])
France	National EPR scheme (Cyclamed)	Article 32 of the law n°2007-248	Mandatory EPR-scheme, Retail pharmacies act as collection sites	Industry	(RiSKWa, 2016[142])
Germany	Some voluntary take-back schemes on local level	Generally, it is recommended to dispose pharmaceutical waste via the household bin, as MSW is incinerated			
Hungary	National EPR scheme (Recyclomed)	National system for the collection and disposal of household pharmaceuticals since 2005 (20/2005. [VI.10])	Collection bins at pharmacies and other medicine outlets (e.g. petrol stations)	EPR, financed by the pharmaceutical industry, as a percentage of sales proportion of the previous year	(Health Care Without Harm, 2013[143])
Iceland	National level programme	Mandatory obligation of pharmacies to participate in the take-back scheme	Pharmacies		
Ireland	Pharmacies are expected to accept any medicines returned	Retail Pharmacy Businesses Regulations 2008	Via pharmacies and take back initiatives (DUMP - Dispose of Unused Medicine Properly)	Largely by pharmacies	(Pharmaceutical Society Ireland, 2017[144])
Israel		No legislation for pharmaceutical waste in place	Pharmacies are expected to accept medicines from the public.	Government (Israeli Ministry of Health)	(Barnett-Itzhaki et al., 2016[86])
Italy	National EPR scheme (Assinde)	Decree D.P.R. 254/2003 specifies that expired drugs, as well as cytotoxic and cytostatic drugs must be collected and incinerated, financed by producers	Collection bins are available in pharmacies, healthcare centres, on streets or at hazardous waste collection sites	Pharmaceutical industry. In addition, some municipalities organise their own collection systems	(PGEU, 2021[145])
Japan	Some voluntary take-back schemes on local level or within businesses				
Korea	National voluntary programme		Voluntary take-back by some pharmacies	Self-funded by pharmacies	
Latvia	Voluntary collection by pharmacies	No legislation in place	Pharmacies and hazardous waste collection centres		(Methonen et al., 2020[87])
Lithuania	Collection by Pharmacies	Community pharmacies are obliged to accept UEM and send them for safe disposal (Farmacijos istatymas nustato 2006/6/22 d. No. X 709, Official Gazette, 2006, Number: 78-3056)	Pharmacies	Pharmacies cover costs of collection. Government responsible for financing disposal.	(Methonen et al., 2020[87])

Country	System	Legislation	Collection method	Funding	Reference
Luxembourg	"Superdreckskëscht": collection system in co-operation with pharmacies		Waste can be returned to community pharmacies, to mobile collection centres from the Ministry of Environment, or to recycling centres directly	Government funded treatment facilities	(SuperDrecksKëscht, 2020[146])
Mexico	"SINGREM" take-back scheme in 25 out of 32 states	Article 28 of waste prevention law (LGPGIR – 2006) requires the pharmaceutical industry to define and execute a waste management plan for UEM		Organised and financed by the National Chamber of the Pharmaceutical Industry (CANIFARMA)	(Singrem, 2018[130])
New Zealand	Voluntary programme by community pharmacies			Pharmacies, sometimes compensated by district health boards	(Anthony Roberts, 2015[147])
Norway	National drug take-back system	Mandatory legislation for pharmacies to receive drugs at no costs to the consumer			(Helsenorge, n.d.[148])
Poland	Voluntary collection points in some pharmacies, otherwise municipal offices and health care centres	Act on Maintaining Municipalities Clean and in Order of 13 September 1996, i.e. (Journal of Laws of 2020 item 1439, as amended)	Waste can be returned to waste collection points or pharmacies	Municipalities are required to collect UEM at least in civic amenity sites	(Rogowska et al., 2019[110])
Portugal	National collection system (SIGREM)	National legislation since 2001	Pharmacies	Funded through an EPR by the pharmaceutical industry	(Health Care Without Harm, 2013[143])
Slovakia	Mandatory legislation in place		Pharmacies are required to take back unused medicine and hand it to the State Institute for Drug Control, which deals with its proper treatment and disposal. Municipalities need to provide information on the system	Financed by the State Institute for Drug Control	(State institute for drug control, 2020[149])
Slovenia	Compulsory take back system	Decree on the management of waste medicine (Official Gazette RS, Nos. 105/08 and 84/18 - ZIURKOE)	UEM can be returned to municipal collection centres for hazardous waste, pharmacies or during collection campaigns	Medicine wholesaler is liable to fund treatment of UEM	(Official Gazzette of the Republic of Slovenia, 2008[150])

MANAGEMENT OF PHARMACEUTICAL HOUSEHOLD WASTE © OECD 2022

Country	Scheme	Legislation	Collection	Funding / responsibility	Reference
Spain	National EPR scheme (SIGRE)		Pharmacies	PRO funded by pharmaceutical companies.	(SIGRE, 2018[151])
Sweden	National EPR scheme (financed and organised individually by retail pharmacies)		Mandatory EPR-scheme, retail pharmacies commonly act as collection sites and organise collection independently	Pharmacies are considered the "producer" in the Swedish EPR	
Switzerland	Return scheme in place (depending on Canton)	Pharmaceutical waste shall be collected separately	Pharmacies or designated disposal points	In some Cantons the system is government-funded, in others pharmacies bear the cost	(Federal Office for the Environment, 2021[152])
The Netherlands	Locally organised voluntary collection by pharmacies	Environmental Management Act: declares that municipalities are responsible for the collection and processing of medical waste	Collection points in pharmacies	Municipalities generally cover the cost of disposal, though in 19 out of 355 municipalities (6%) pharmacies still bear the costs	(KNMP, 2020[109])
Turkey	Voluntary collection by pharmacies (through ÇEKOOP)	No legislation in place			
United States	25 local EPR laws in the US; 3 at state-level, 18 at county-level and 4 at city-level		Either voluntary programs by firms or governments, or mandatory programs through EPR	Governmental, firms or by industry	
United Kingdom	Pharmacies are obliged to take back and sort unused medicine and return them to National Health Services	The National Health Service (Pharmaceutical and Local Pharmaceutical Services) Regulations, 2013	Collection in Pharmacies and through local collection events	Local government funds the treatment process	(Paut Kusturica, Tomas and Sabo, 2016[96])

Notes

[1] Nevertheless, hospital effluents may play an important role in the introduction of pathogens into public wastewaters, especially concerning multi-resistant bacteria. To date, most hospitals are not specifically equipped with wastewater treatment infrastructure to immediately treat their highly concentrated effluent after discharge.

[2] Note that this report focuses on discharge from *human* pharmaceuticals. However, pharmaceuticals for veterinary use, aquaculture and agriculture form an important source of pharmaceutical residues in the environment and are included here for completeness.

[3] Many of the antimicrobial resistant bacteria emerge in hospitals and their presence in hospital effluents is thus disproportionate (Rizzo et al., 2013[153]; Hocquet, Muller and Bertrand, 2016[154]).

[4] In some countries, studies have identified high concentrations of APIs in the discharge vicinities of pharmaceutical production facilities (Lübbert et al., 2017[155]; Larsson, 2014[156]).

[5] See (OECD, 2019[3]) for a more detailed discussion of proven and potential environmental and health effects of pharmaceuticals.

[6] A recent report cites this value (BIO Intelligence Service, 2013[7]), which was initially given by a representative of the pharmaceutical industry, during the Workshop on the presence of medicinal products in the environment held in Brussels by BIO IS on behalf of EAHC, on 19 September 2012.

[7] UEM was considered preventable when 1) larger amounts of medication were prescribed than needed for the expected duration of use; 2) excessive medication amounts were prescribed for a terminal patient; 3) a pharmacist dispensed more than the prescribed amount; 4) in case of a prescription error (e.g. wrong strength prescribed); 5) a refill that was no longer needed was dispensed; or 6) patients had side effects or insufficient effect of treatment at the moment of a refill, but still collected the medication.

[8] In the study, returned medicines were considered eligible for re-dispensing when all of the following criteria were met: 1) the package was unopened; 2) the package was undamaged; and 3) there was at least 6 months between the return date and the expiry date.

[9] Some pharmaceuticals, such as cytostatic and cytotoxic pharmaceuticals are classified as hazardous waste and are not covered by the scheme. Municipalities are responsible for collection, transport and disposal of hazardous wastes from households.

[10] Based on an interview with the Swedish Pharmacy Association.

[11] The 2010 "Drug Disposal Act" made it possible for public and private entities to develop secure and convenient collection and disposal systems and encourages them to do so on a voluntary basis (US Government, 2010[157]).

[12] The "FDA flush list" indicates a list of 13 active pharmaceutical ingredients that can be disposed by a household by flushing if no drug take-back program is available. Flushing in these instances is endorsed to limit accidental poisoning and potential exposure to children and pets. According to FDA the risk of accidental exposure outweighs the environmental harm of flushing for all pharmaceuticals on the list (FDA, 2020[127]). The FDA maintains that the best disposal option for all pharmaceuticals, including those on the flush list, is via drug-take-back programs.

[13] Uncertainty exists about how much of the medicines bought are entering the waste stream. This indicator thus needs to be interpreted with caution.

[14] For instance, in the Netherlands, municipalities generally cover the costs of disposal for pharmacies, though in 19 out of 355 Dutch municipalities (6%), pharmacies need to bear the costs themselves (KNMP, 2020[109]).

[15] See the OECD Working Paper *Extended Producer Responsibility (EPR) and the Impact of Online Sales* for more specific guidance on this topic (Hilton et al., 2019[158]).

[16] Each of these approaches and possible policy initiatives are discussed more extensively in the OECD report on *Pharmaceutical Residues in Freshwater* (OECD, 2019[3]).

[17] The *OECD Updated EPR Guidance for Efficient Waste Management* provides more specific guidance on designing EPR systems (OECD, 2016[114]).

[18] The OECD Working Paper *Extended Producer Responsibility (EPR) and the Impact of Online Sales* provides more specific guidance on this topic (Hilton et al., 2019[158]).

[19] In the EU, Directive 2004/27/EC (Article 54j) states that "reference to any appropriate collection system in place shall appear on the outer packaging of medicinal products or, where there is no outer packaging, on the immediate packaging".

References

Alnahas, F. et al. (2020), "Expired Medication: Societal, Regulatory and Ethical Aspects of a Wasted Opportunity", *International Journal of Environmental Research and Public Health*, Vol. 17/3, p. 787, https://doi.org/10.3390/ijerph17030787. [94]

Amanda J. Wheeler, Fiona Kelly, Jean Spinks, E. (2016), *National Return and Disposal of Unwanted Medicines Project Audit 2016*, Griffith University, https://returnmed.com.au/wp-content/uploads/2017/08/NatRUM-Project-Final-Report-Griffith-University.pdf. [84]

Anthony Roberts (2015), *SUBMISSION ON PHARMACEUTICAL WASTE MANAGEMENT*, https://www.parliament.nz/resource/en-nz/51SCHE_EVI_51DBHOH_PET63223_1_A448630/403a29a2be0a6d14998f70bdb7a100c1 6f7c12bc (accessed on 12 March 2020). [147]

Araújo, A. et al. (2019), "Anti-cancer drugs in aquatic environment can cause cancer: Insight about mutagenicity in tadpoles", *Science of The Total Environment*, Vol. 650, pp. 2284-2293, https://doi.org/10.1016/J.SCITOTENV.2018.09.373. [47]

Armstrong, B. et al. (2016), "Reproductive effects in fathead minnows (Pimphales promelas) following a 21 d exposure to 17α-ethinylestradiol", *Chemosphere*, Vol. 144, pp. 366-373, https://doi.org/10.1016/j.chemosphere.2015.08.078. [66]

Bach, P. et al. (2016), "Overspending driven by oversized single dose vials of cancer drugs", *BMJ*, p. i788, https://doi.org/10.1136/bmj.i788. [14]

Barnett-Itzhaki, Z. et al. (2016), "Household medical waste disposal policy in Israel", *Israel Journal of Health Policy Research*, Vol. 5/1, https://doi.org/10.1186/s13584-016-0108-1. [86]

Behera, S. et al. (2011), "Occurrence and removal of antibiotics, hormones and several other pharmaceuticals in wastewater treatment plants of the largest industrial city of Korea", *Science of The Total Environment*, Vol. 409/20, pp. 4351-4360, https://doi.org/10.1016/J.SCITOTENV.2011.07.015. [22]

Bekker, C. et al. (2018), "Patient and medication factors associated with preventable medication waste and possibilities for redispensing", *International Journal of Clinical Pharmacy*, Vol. 40/3, pp. 704-711, https://doi.org/10.1007/s11096-018-0642-8. [98]

Belgian Pharmacy Association (2016), *Breng uw vervallen of ongebruikte geneesmiddelen terug naar de apotheek! | Apotheek.be*, https://apotheekwelle.be/breng-vervallen-of-ongebruikte-medicatie-naar-onze-apotheek/ (accessed on 12 October 2020). [128]

Berninger, J. et al. (2011), "Effects of the antihistamine diphenhydramine on selected aquatic organisms", *Environmental Toxicology and Chemistry*, Vol. 30/9, pp. 2065-2072, https://doi.org/10.1002/etc.590. [56]

Bettington, E. et al. (2018), "When is a medicine unwanted, how is it disposed, and how might safe disposal be promoted? Insights from the Australian population", *Australian Health Review*, Vol. 42/6, p. 709, https://doi.org/10.1071/ah16296. [112]

BIO Intelligence Service (2013), *Study on the environmental risks of medicinal products, Final Report prepared for Executive Agency for Health and Consumers*, BIO Intelligence Service, Paris, https://ec.europa.eu/health/sites/health/files/files/environment/study_environment.pdf. [7]

Bound, J. and N. Voulvoulis (2005), "Household Disposal of Pharmaceuticals as a Pathway for Aquatic Contamination in the United Kingdom", *Environmental Health Perspectives*, Vol. 113/12, pp. 1705-1711, https://doi.org/10.1289/ehp.8315. [80]

Brain, R. et al. (2008), "Aquatic plants exposed to pharmaceuticals: effects and risks", *Reviews of environmental contamination and toxicology*, Vol. 192, pp. 67-115, http://www.ncbi.nlm.nih.gov/pubmed/18020304 (accessed on 27 June 2019). [44]

Braund, R., B. Peake and L. Shieffelbien (2009), "Disposal practices for unused medications in New Zealand", *Environment International*, Vol. 35/6, pp. 952-955, https://doi.org/10.1016/j.envint.2009.04.003. [91]

British Columbia (2017), *Environmental Management Act - RECYCLING REGULATION*, http://www.bclaws.ca/civix/document/id/crbc/crbc/449_2004 (accessed on 3 August 2018). [122]

Brodin, T. et al. (2013), "Dilute Concentrations of a Psychiatric Drug Alter Behavior of Fish from Natural Populations", *Science*, Vol. 339/6121, pp. 814-815, https://doi.org/10.1126/science.1226850. [5]

Brodin, T. et al. (2014), "Ecological effects of pharmaceuticals in aquatic systems—impacts through behavioural alterations", *Philosophical Transactions of the Royal Society B: Biological Sciences*, Vol. 369/1656, https://doi.org/10.1098/rstb.2013.0580. [69]

Bui, X. et al. (2016), "Multicriteria assessment of advanced treatment technologies for micropollutants removal at large-scale applications", *Science of The Total Environment*, Vol. 563-564, pp. 1050-1067, https://doi.org/10.1016/j.scitotenv.2016.04.191. [25]

Burns, E. et al. (2018), "Application of prioritization approaches to optimize environmental monitoring and testing of pharmaceuticals", *Journal of Toxicology and Environmental Health, Part B*, Vol. 21/3, pp. 115-141, https://doi.org/10.1080/10937404.2018.1465873. [2]

Business Fortune Insights (2019), *Global ePharmacy Market Size, Share & Growth Analysis, 2026*, https://www.fortunebusinessinsights.com/industry-reports/epharmacy-market-100238 (accessed on 25 February 2020). [132]

Caldwell, D. et al. (2019), "Environmental risk assessment of metformin and its transformation product guanylurea: II. Occurrence in surface waters of Europe and the United States and derivation of predicted no-effect concentrations", *Chemosphere*, Vol. 216, pp. 855-865, https://doi.org/10.1016/J.CHEMOSPHERE.2018.10.038. [76]

Campos, B. et al. (2016), "Depressing Antidepressant: Fluoxetine Affects Serotonin Neurons Causing Adverse Reproductive Responses in Daphnia magna", *Environmental Science and Technology*, Vol. 50/11, pp. 6000-6007, https://doi.org/10.1021/acs.est.6b00826. [74]

Česen, M. et al. (2016), "Ecotoxicity and genotoxicity of cyclophosphamide, ifosfamide, their metabolites/transformation products and their mixtures", *Environmental Pollution*, Vol. 210, pp. 192-201, https://doi.org/10.1016/j.envpol.2015.12.017. [45]

Clarke, B. et al. (2015), "Investigating landfill leachate as a source of trace organic pollutants", *Chemosphere*, Vol. 127, pp. 269-275, https://doi.org/10.1016/j.chemosphere.2015.02.030. [30]

Crago, J. et al. (2016), "Age-dependent effects in fathead minnows from the anti-diabetic drug metformin", *General and Comparative Endocrinology*, Vol. 232, pp. 185-190, https://doi.org/10.1016/j.ygcen.2015.12.030. [50]

CSA (2018), *Etude sur le gisement des Médicaments Non Utilisés (MNU*, https://www.csa.eu/fr/survey/etude-sur-le-gisement-des-medicaments-non-utilises-mnu (accessed on 16 May 2019). [117]

Cyclamed (2019), *Cyclamed - annual report for 2018*, https://www.cyclamed.org (accessed on 16 May 2019). [82]

De Castro-Català, N. et al. (2017), "Evidence of low dose effects of the antidepressant fluoxetine and the fungicide prochloraz on the behavior of the keystone freshwater invertebrate Gammarus pulex", *Environmental Pollution*, Vol. 231, pp. 406-414, https://doi.org/10.1016/j.envpol.2017.07.088. [72]

de Oliveira, L. et al. (2016), "Acute and chronic ecotoxicological effects of four pharmaceuticals drugs on cladoceran Daphnia magna", *Drug and Chemical Toxicology*, Vol. 39/1, pp. 13-21, https://doi.org/10.3109/01480545.2015.1029048. [62]

DEA (2022), *National Take Back Day Results*, https://takebackday.dea.gov/ (accessed on 5 May 2021). [126]

DEA (2020), *How to properly dispose of your unused medicines*, https://www.dea.gov/sites/default/files/2018-10/Proper%20Disposal%20Flier%20%28October%202018%29.pdf. [103]

Di Poi, C. et al. (2014), "Cryptic and biochemical responses of young cuttlefish Sepia officinalis exposed to environmentally relevant concentrations of fluoxetine", *Aquatic Toxicology*, Vol. 151, pp. 36-45, https://doi.org/10.1016/j.aquatox.2013.12.026. [73]

DSI (2019), 환경오염유발의 폐의약품 처리실태와 개선에 관한 기초 연구 *("Basic research on the status and improvement of waste medicines that cause environmental pollution")*, https://www.dsi.re.kr/board.es?mid=a10101000000&bid=0001&list_no=18687&act=view (accessed on 8 March 2022). [88]

Dutch Sustainable Pharmacy Coalition (2020), *Effecten van een pilot inzamelweek : ongebruikte medicijnen terug naar de apotheek*, https://www.vereniginginnovatievegeneesmiddelen.nl/nieuwsberichten/2020/09/website/meeste-nederlanders-houden-medicijnen-over. [133]

Dutch Waste Sector (2018), *Amsterdam hospital AMC purifies and re-uses wastewater with Pharmafilter*, https://www.dutchwatersector.com/news/amsterdam-hospital-amc-purifies-and-re-uses-wastewater-with-pharmafilter (accessed on 7 August 2020). [26]

EC (2016), *Fate and effects of cytostatic pharmaceuticals in the environment and the identification of biomarkers for and improved risk assessment on environmental exposure*, European Commission, Brussels, https://cordis.europa.eu/project/rcn/96703/brief/en. [48]

Efosa, N. et al. (2017), "Diclofenac can exhibit estrogenic modes of action in male Xenopus laevis, and affects the hypothalamus-pituitary-gonad axis and mating vocalizations", *Chemosphere*, Vol. 173, pp. 69-77, https://doi.org/10.1016/j.chemosphere.2017.01.030. [41]

EU JRC (2019), *Best Available Techniques (BAT) Reference Document for Waste Treatment Industries*, https://eippcb.jrc.ec.europa.eu/sites/default/files/2020-01/JRC118637_WI_Bref_2019_published_0.pdf. [107]

EurEau (2019), *Treating micropollutants at waste water treatment plants: Experiences and developments from European countries*, http://www.eureau.org/resources/briefing-notes/3826-briefing-note-on-treating-micropollutants-at-the-wwtp/file (accessed on 29 September 2020). [27]

European Commission (2004), *DIRECTIVE 2004/27/EC OF THE EUROPEAN PARLIAMENT AND OF THE COUNCIL*, European Commission, Brussels, https://eur-lex.europa.eu/legal-content/EN/TXT/PDF/?uri=CELEX:32004L0027&from=EN (accessed on 3 August 2021). [104]

European Commission (2000), "Commission Decision 2000/532/EC", https://eur-lex.europa.eu/legal-content/EN/TXT/?uri=CELEX:02000D0532-20150601 (accessed on 12 October 2020). [108]

Eurostat (2020), *Municipal waste statistics*, https://ec.europa.eu/eurostat/statistics-explained/index.php/Municipal_waste_statistics (accessed on 12 October 2020). [83]

FASS (2020), *FASS Allmänhet - Startsida*, https://www.fass.se/LIF/startpage (accessed on 20 February 2020). [137]

FDA (2020), *Drug Disposal: Flush Potentially Dangerous Medicine*, https://www.fda.gov/drugs/disposal-unused-medicines-what-you-should-know/drug-disposal-flush-potentially-dangerous-medicine (accessed on 6 August 2020). [127]

Federal Office for the Environment (2021), *Entsorgung von medizinischen Abfällen*, https://www.bafu.admin.ch/bafu/de/home/themen/abfall/publikationen-studien/publikationen/entsorgung-von-medizinischen-abfaellen.html (accessed on 29 April 2022). [152]

Ferrari, B. et al. (2003), "Ecotoxicological impact of pharmaceuticals found in treated wastewaters: study of carbamazepine, clofibric acid, and diclofenac", *Ecotoxicology and Environmental Safety*, Vol. 55/3, pp. 359-370, https://doi.org/10.1016/s0147-6513(02)00082-9. [52]

Ferreira da Silva, M. et al. (2007), "Antimicrobial resistance patterns in Enterobacteriaceae isolated from an urban wastewater treatment plant", *FEMS Microbiology Ecology*, Vol. 60/1, pp. 166-176, https://doi.org/10.1111/j.1574-6941.2006.00268.x. [8]

Finnish Pharmacy Association (2016), *Lääkejätettä syntyy jopa 100 miljoonan euron arvosta vuodessa - Suomen Apteekkariliitto*, https://www.apteekkariliitto.fi/media/tiedotteet/2016/laakejatetta-syntyy-jopa-100-miljoonan-euron-arvosta-vuodessa.html (accessed on 12 October 2020). [78]

Garric, J. et al. (2007), "Effects of the parasiticide ivermectin on the cladoceran Daphnia magna and the green alga Pseudokirchneriella subcapitata", *Chemosphere*, Vol. 69/6, pp. 903-910, https://doi.org/10.1016/j.chemosphere.2007.05.070. [60]

German Environment Agency (2019), *The database "Pharmaceuticals in the Environment"-Update and new analysis Final report*, https://www.umweltbundesamt.de/en/publikationen/the-database-pharmaceuticals-in-the-environment (accessed on 21 February 2020). [4]

Giltrow, E. et al. (2009), "Chronic effects assessment and plasma concentrations of the β-blocker propranolol in fathead minnows (Pimephales promelas)", *Aquatic Toxicology*, Vol. 95/3, pp. 195-202, https://doi.org/10.1016/j.aquatox.2009.09.002. [61]

Götz, K. and F. Keil (2007), "Medikamentenentsorgung in privaten Haushalten: Ein Faktor bei der Gewässerbelastung mit Arzneimittelwirkstoffen?", *Umweltwissenschaften und Schadstoff-Forschung*, Vol. 19/3, pp. 180-188, https://doi.org/10.1065/uwsf2007.07.201. [97]

Government Manitoba (2010), *Household Hazardous Material and Prescribed Material Stewardship Regulation*, https://web2.gov.mb.ca/laws/regs/annual/2010/016.pdf (accessed on 3 August 2020). [119]

Government Ontario (2014), *O. Reg. 298/12: COLLECTION OF PHARMACEUTICALS AND SHARPS - RESPONSIBILITIES OF PRODUCERS*, https://www.ontario.ca/laws/regulation/120298 (accessed on 3 August 2018). [120]

Guo, J., A. Boxall and K. Selby (2015), "Do pharmaceuticals pose a threat to primary producers?", *Critical Reviews in Environmental Science and Technology*, Vol. 45/23, https://doi.org/10.1080/10643389.2015.1061873. [43]

Gyllenhammar, I. et al. (2009), "Reproductive toxicity in Xenopus tropicalis after developmental exposure to environmental concentrations of ethynylestradiol", *Aquatic Toxicology*, Vol. 91/2, pp. 171-178, https://doi.org/10.1016/j.aquatox.2008.06.019. [65]

Health Care Without Harm (2013), *Unused Pharmaceuticals Where Do They End Up? A Snapshot of European Collection Schemes*, https://noharm-europe.org/sites/default/files/documents-files/4646/2013-12%20Unused%20pharmaceuticals.pdf. [143]

Helsenorge (n.d.), *Retur av medisin - helsenorge.no*, https://helsenorge.no/legemidler/oppbevaring-holdbarhet-retur/levere-gamle-medisiner (accessed on 12 March 2020). [148]

Hilton, M. et al. (2019), "Extended Producer Responsibility (EPR) and the Impact of Online Sales", *OECD Environment Working Papers*, No. 142, OECD Publishing, Paris, https://doi.org/10.1787/cde28569-en. [158]

Hocquet, D., A. Muller and X. Bertrand (2016), "What happens in hospitals does not stay in hospitals: antibiotic-resistant bacteria in hospital wastewater systems", *Journal of Hospital Infection*, Vol. 93/4, pp. 395-402, https://doi.org/10.1016/j.jhin.2016.01.010. [154]

Hollender, J. et al. (2009), "Elimination of Organic Micropollutants in a Municipal Wastewater Treatment Plant Upgraded with a Full-Scale Post-Ozonation Followed by Sand Filtration", *Environmental Science & Technology*, Vol. 43/20, pp. 7862-7869, https://doi.org/10.1021/es9014629. [23]

HPSA (2020), *Provincial Documents*, https://healthsteward.ca/about/provincial-documents/. [123]

Hughes, A. et al. (2016), "Prescription Drug Use and Misuse in the United States: Results from the 2015 National Survey on Drug Use and Health", *National Survey on Drug Use and Health*, http://article.psychiatrist.com/?ContentType=START&ID=10002608. [10]

Janusinfro (2022), *Pharmaceuticals and Environment - Classification*, https://janusinfo.se/beslutsstod/lakemedelochmiljo/pharmaceuticalsandenvironment/environment/classification.5.7b57ecc216251fae47488423.html (accessed on 28 April 2022). [136]

Jonsson, M. et al. (2014), "Antihistamines and aquatic insects: Bioconcentration and impacts on behavior in damselfly larvae (Zygoptera)", *Science of the Total Environment*, Vol. 472, pp. 108-111, https://doi.org/10.1016/j.scitotenv.2013.10.104. [58]

Kellner, M. et al. (2016), "Waterborne citalopram has anxiolytic effects and increases locomotor activity in the three-spine stickleback (Gasterosteus aculeatus)", *Aquatic Toxicology*, Vol. 173, pp. 19-28, https://doi.org/10.1016/j.aquatox.2015.12.026. [70]

Kelly, F. et al. (2018), "'You don't throw these things out:' an exploration of medicines retention and disposal practices in Australian homes", *BMC Public Health*, Vol. 18/1, https://doi.org/10.1186/s12889-018-5753-6. [113]

Kennedy-Hendricks, A. et al. (2016), "Medication Sharing, Storage, and Disposal Practices for Opioid Medications Among US Adults", *JAMA Internal Medicine*, Vol. 176/7, p. 1027, https://doi.org/10.1001/jamainternmed.2016.2543. [79]

Kidd, K. et al. (2007), "Collapse of a fish population after exposure to a synthetic estrogen", *Proceedings of the National Academy of Sciences of the United States of America*, Vol. 104/21, pp. 8897-8901, https://doi.org/10.1073/pnas.0609568104. [63]

KNMP (2020), *KNMP onderzoek - inzameling medicijnafval 2020*, https://www.knmp.nl/dossiers/duurzame-zorg/medicijnafval (accessed on 7 August 2020). [109]

Kristofco, L. et al. (2016), "Age matters: Developmental stage of Danio rerio larvae influences photomotor response thresholds to diazinion or diphenhydramine", *Aquatic Toxicology*, Vol. 170, pp. 344-354, https://doi.org/10.1016/J.AQUATOX.2015.09.011. [57]

Kruopienė, J. and J. Dvarionienė (2010), "Management of Environmental Risks in the Life Cycle of Human Pharmaceuticals in Lithuania", Vol. 52/2, http://erem.ktu.lt/index.php/erem/article/view/77 (accessed on 6 August 2020). [89]

Kümmerer, K. (2009), "The presence of pharmaceuticals in the environment due to human use – present knowledge and future challenges", *Journal of Environmental Management*, Vol. 90/8, pp. 2354-2366, https://doi.org/10.1016/j.jenvman.2009.01.023. [16]

Kümmerer, K. and M. Hempel (2010), *Green and Sustainable Pharmacy*, Springer, Berlin, Heidelberg, https://doi.org/10.1007/978-3-642-05199-9. [21]

Küster, A. and N. Adler (2014), "Pharmaceuticals in the environment: scientific evidence of risks and its regulation", *Philosophical Transactions of the Royal Society B: Biological Sciences*, Vol. 369/1656, p. 20130587, https://doi.org/10.1098/rstb.2013.0587. [36]

Kvarnryd, M. et al. (2011), "Early life progestin exposure causes arrested oocyte development, oviductal agenesis and sterility in adult Xenopus tropicalis frogs", *Aquatic Toxicology*, Vol. 103/1-2, pp. 18-24, https://doi.org/10.1016/j.aquatox.2011.02.003. [64]

Lapworth, D. et al. (2012), "Emerging organic contaminants in groundwater: A review of sources, fate and occurrence", *Environmental Pollution*, Vol. 163, pp. 287-303, https://doi.org/10.1016/j.envpol.2011.12.034. [17]

Larsson, D. (2014), "Pollution from drug manufacturing: review and perspectives", *Philosophical Transactions of the Royal Society B: Biological Sciences*, Vol. 369/1656, p. 20130571, https://doi.org/10.1098/rstb.2013.0571. [156]

Larsson, J. and L. Lööf (2016), *Medicines in the environment | Läkemedelsboken*, https://lakemedelsboken.se/kapitel/lakemedelsanvandning/lakemedel_i_miljon.html (accessed on 21 February 2020). [20]

Law, A. et al. (2015), "Taking stock of medication wastage: Unused medications in US households", *Research in Social and Administrative Pharmacy*, Vol. 11/4, pp. 571-578, https://doi.org/10.1016/j.sapharm.2014.10.003. [13]

Lazzara, R. et al. (2012), "Low environmental levels of fluoxetine induce spawning and changes in endogenous estradiol levels in the zebra mussel Dreissena polymorpha", *Aquatic Toxicology*, Vol. 106-107, pp. 123-130, https://doi.org/10.1016/j.aquatox.2011.11.003. [75]

Legifrance (2021), *Arrêté du 22 décembre 2021 portant agrément d'un éco-organisme de la filière à responsabilité élargie des producteurs de médicaments*, https://www.legifrance.gouv.fr/download/pdf?id=tuJ-YzZKSB-nAqvlqBHix2WUgvYvfJ3GciREwkWtl3E=. [116]

Legifrance (2007), *LOI n° 2007-248 du 26 février 2007 portant diverses dispositions d'adaptation au droit communautaire dans le domaine du médicament | Legifrance*, https://www.legifrance.gouv.fr/affichTexte.do?cidTexte=JORFTEXT000000613381&dateTexte=&categorieLien=id. [115]

Lübbert, C. et al. (2017), "Environmental pollution with antimicrobial agents from bulk drug manufacturing industries in Hyderabad, South India, is associated with dissemination of extended-spectrum beta-lactamase and carbapenemase-producing pathogens", *Infection*, Vol. 45/4, pp. 479-491, https://doi.org/10.1007/s15010-017-1007-2. [155]

Lu, M. et al. (2016), "Occurrence and treatment efficiency of pharmaceuticals in landfill leachates", *Waste Management*, Vol. 55, pp. 257-264, https://doi.org/10.1016/j.wasman.2016.03.029. [32]

Martinez, C. et al. (2018), "In vivo study of teratogenic and anticonvulsant effects of antiepileptics drugs in zebrafish embryo and larvae", *Neurotoxicology and Teratology*, Vol. 66, pp. 17-24, https://doi.org/10.1016/j.ntt.2018.01.008. [51]

Masoner, J. et al. (2020), "Landfill leachate contributes per-/poly-fluoroalkyl substances (PFAS) and pharmaceuticals to municipal wastewater", *Environmental Science: Water Research & Technology*, Vol. 6/5, pp. 1300-1311, https://doi.org/10.1039/d0ew00045k. [33]

Masoner, J. et al. (2015), "Landfill leachate as a mirror of today's disposable society: Pharmaceuticals and other contaminants of emerging concern in final leachate from landfills in the conterminous United States", *Environmental Toxicology and Chemistry*, Vol. 35/4, pp. 906-918, https://doi.org/10.1002/etc.3219. [29]

Masoner, J. et al. (2014), "Contaminants of emerging concern in fresh leachate from landfills in the conterminous United States", *Environ. Sci.: Processes Impacts*, Vol. 16/10, pp. 2335-2354, https://doi.org/10.1039/c4em00124a. [18]

Mathias, F. et al. (2018), "Effects of low concentrations of ibuprofen on freshwater fish Rhamdia quelen", *Environmental Toxicology and Pharmacology*, Vol. 59, pp. 105-113, https://doi.org/10.1016/j.etap.2018.03.008. [38]

MedsDisposal (2021), *About us - Meds Disposal*, http://medsdisposal.eu/about-us/ (accessed on 16 March 2021). [134]

Meinertz, J. et al. (2010), "Chronic toxicity of diphenhydramine hydrochloride and erythromycin thiocyanate to Daphnia, Daphnia magna, in a continuous exposure test system", *Bulletin of Environmental Contamination and Toxicology*, Vol. 85/5, pp. 447-451, https://doi.org/10.1007/s00128-010-0117-7. [59]

Melvin, S. and F. Leusch (2016), "Removal of trace organic contaminants from domestic wastewater: A meta-analysis comparison of sewage treatment technologies", *Environment International*, Vol. 92-93, pp. 183-188, https://doi.org/10.1016/J.ENVINT.2016.03.031. [24]

Methonen, J. et al. (2020), *Good practices for take-back and disposal of unused pharmaceuticals in the Baltic Sea region*, Finnish Environment Institute, https://helda.helsinki.fi/bitstream/handle/10138/319009/SYKEre_34_2020_CWPharma.pdf?sequence=4&isAllowed=y. [87]

Mezzelani, M. et al. (2016), "Ecotoxicological potential of non-steroidal anti-inflammatory drugs (NSAIDs) in marine organisms: Bioavailability, biomarkers and natural occurrence in Mytilus galloprovincialis", *Marine Environmental Research*, Vol. 121, pp. 31-39, https://doi.org/10.1016/j.marenvres.2016.03.005. [40]

Moore, S. et al. (2016), "Endogenous Estrogens, Estrogen Metabolites, and Breast Cancer Risk in Postmenopausal Chinese Women", *Journal of the National Cancer Institute*, Vol. 108/10, https://doi.org/10.1093/jnci/djw103. [67]

Musson, S. and T. Townsend (2009), "Pharmaceutical compound content of municipal solid waste", *Journal of Hazardous Materials*, Vol. 162/2-3, pp. 730-735, https://doi.org/10.1016/j.jhazmat.2008.05.089. [81]

Nash, J. et al. (2004), "Long-Term Exposure to Environmental Concentrations of the Pharmaceutical Ethynylestradiol Causes Reproductive Failure in Fish", *Environmental Health Perspectives*, Vol. 112/17, pp. 1725-1733, https://doi.org/10.1289/ehp.7209. [6]

Näslund, J. et al. (2017), "Diclofenac affects kidney histology in the three-spined stickleback (Gasterosteus aculeatus) at low Mg/L concentrations", *Aquatic Toxicology*, Vol. 189, pp. 87-96, https://doi.org/10.1016/j.aquatox.2017.05.017. [37]

NatRUM (2020), *National Return and Disposal of Unwanted Medicines Project*, https://returnmed.com.au/pharmacists (accessed on 23 July 2020). [111]

NaWaM (2020), *Arzneimittel-Entsorgung richtig gemacht*, https://arzneimittelentsorgung.de/home/ (accessed on 24 March 2020). [105]

Nelles, J., W. Hu and G. Prins (2011), "Estrogen action and prostate cancer", *Expert Review of Endocrinology and Metabolism*, Vol. 6/3, pp. 437-451, https://doi.org/10.1586/eem.11.20. [68]

New York Department of Environmental Conservation (2018), *The Feasibility of Creating and Implementing a Statewide Pharmaceutical Stewardship Program in New York State*, https://www.dec.ny.gov/docs/materials_minerals_pdf/pharmastewardshipreport.pdf (accessed on 16 May 2019). [125]

Niemuth, N. et al. (2015), "Metformin exposure at environmentally relevant concentrations causes potential endocrine disruption in adult male fish", *Environmental Toxicology and Chemistry*, Vol. 34/2, pp. 291-296, https://doi.org/10.1002/etc.2793. [49]

OECD (2021), *Health at a Glance 2021: OECD Indicators*, OECD Publishing, Paris, https://doi.org/10.1787/ae3016b9-en. [1]

OECD (2019), *Pharmaceutical Residues in Freshwater: Hazards and Policy Responses*, OECD Studies on Water, OECD Publishing, Paris, https://doi.org/10.1787/c936f42d-en. [3]

OECD (2019), "Water: Sewage sludge production and disposal (Edition 2019)", *OECD Environment Statistics* (database), https://doi.org/10.1787/1900ef98-en (accessed on 12 April 2022). [28]

OECD (2018), *Stemming the Superbug Tide: Just A Few Dollars More*, OECD Health Policy Studies, OECD Publishing, Paris, https://doi.org/10.1787/9789264307599-en. [9]

OECD (2016), *Extended Producer Responsibility: Updated Guidance for Efficient Waste Management*, https://doi.org/10.1111/jiec.12022. [114]

Oesterreich.gv.at (2022), *Problemstoffe*, https://www.oesterreich.gv.at/themen/bauen_wohnen_und_umwelt/abfall/Problemstoffe.html (accessed on 29 April 2022). [138]

Official Gazzette of the Republic of Slovenia (2008), *Regulation on the management of waste medicines*, http://www.pisrs.si/Pis.web/pregledPredpisa?id=URED4793# (accessed on 12 March 2020). [150]

PANS (2019), *The Medication Disposal Program*, https://pans.ns.ca/public/programs/medication-disposal (accessed on 17 February 2020). [124]

Paut Kusturica, M., A. Tomas and A. Sabo (2016), "Disposal of Unused Drugs: Knowledge and Behavior Among People Around the World", in *Reviews of Environmental Contamination and Toxicology Volume 240, Reviews of Environmental Contamination and Toxicology*, Springer International Publishing, Cham, https://doi.org/10.1007/398_2016_3. [96]

Persson, M., E. Sabelström and B. Gunnarsson (2009), "Handling of unused prescription drugs — knowledge, behaviour and attitude among Swedish people", *Environment International*, Vol. 35/5, pp. 771-774, https://doi.org/10.1016/j.envint.2008.10.002. [93]

PGEU (2021), *Best Practice Paper on Green and Sustainable Pharmacy in Europe*, https://www.pgeu.eu/publications/pgeu-best-practice-paper-on-green-and-sustainable-pharmacy-in-europe/ (accessed on 25 April 2022). [145]

Pharmaceutical Society Ireland (2017), *Guidelines on the Disposal of Medicinal Products for a Retail Pharmacy Business to Facilitate Compliance with Regulations 4(5) and 6(3) of the Regulation of Retail Pharmacy Businesses Regulations 2008*, https://www.thepsi.ie/Libraries/Folder_Pharmacy_Practice_Guidance/01_5_Disposal_of_Medicinal_Products_for_Retail.sflb.ashx (accessed on 12 March 2020). [144]

PharmaSwap (2022), *What is PharmaSwap?*, https://www.pharmaswap.com/what-is-pharmaswap.html (accessed on 2 March 2022). [99]

Porsbring, T. et al. (2009), "Toxicity of the pharmaceutical clotrimazole to marine microalgal communities", *Aquatic Toxicology*, Vol. 91/3, pp. 203-211, https://doi.org/10.1016/J.AQUATOX.2008.11.003. [54]

Prescription Promise (2020), *Prescription Promise - About Us*, https://rxpromise.wordpress.com/home/about-us/ (accessed on 7 August 2020). [100]

Prince Edward Island Government (2015), *ENVIRONMENTAL PROTECTION ACT MATERIALS STEWARDSHIP AND RECYCLING REGULATIONS*, https://www.princeedwardisland.ca/en/legislation/environmental-protection-act/materials-stewardship-and-recycling-regulations (accessed on 3 August 2019). [121]

Recyclomed (2019), *REPORT on communal pharmaceutical waste collecting 2019*, http://www.recyclomed.hu/images/dokumentumok/report2019-EN.pdf (accessed on 11 August 2020). [129]

Reitsma, M. et al. (2013), *Een derde van de geneesmiddelengebruikers houdt geneesmiddelen over.*, https://nivel.nl/sites/default/files/bestanden/Factsheet-medicijnen-over.pdf (accessed on 19 February 2020). [90]

RiSKWa (2016), *Home - Arzneimittel-Entsorgung richtig gemacht*, https://arzneimittelentsorgung.de/home/ (accessed on 12 March 2020). [142]

Rizzo, L. et al. (2013), "Urban wastewater treatment plants as hotspots for antibiotic resistant bacteria and genes spread into the environment: A review", *Science of The Total Environment*, Vol. 447, pp. 345-360, https://doi.org/10.1016/j.scitotenv.2013.01.032. [153]

Rogowska, J. et al. (2019), "Pharmaceutical Household Waste Practices: Preliminary Findings from a Case Study in Poland", *Environmental Management*, Vol. 64/1, pp. 97-106, https://doi.org/10.1007/s00267-019-01174-7. [110]

Roose-Amsaleg, C. and A. Laverman (2016), "Do antibiotics have environmental side-effects? Impact of synthetic antibiotics on biogeochemical processes", *Environmental Science and Pollution Research*, Vol. 23/5, pp. 4000-4012, https://doi.org/10.1007/s11356-015-4943-3. [42]

Ruhoy, I. and C. Daughton (2008), "Beyond the medicine cabinet: An analysis of where and why medications accumulate", *Environment International*, Vol. 34/8, pp. 1157-1169, https://doi.org/10.1016/j.envint.2008.05.002. [77]

SaferX (2017), *DUMP (Disposal of Unwanted Medicines Properly) campaign | SafeRx*, http://www.saferx.co.nz/brief-updates/dump-campaign/ (accessed on 16 March 2020). [135]

SAMHSA (2019), "Key substance use and mental health indicators in the United States: Results from the 2018 National Survey on Drug Use and Health", *HHS Publication No. PEP19-5068, NSDUH Series H-54*, Vol. 170, pp. 51-58, https://doi.org/10.1016/j.drugalcdep.2016.10.042. [12]

Santos, L. et al. (2010), "Ecotoxicological aspects related to the presence of pharmaceuticals in the aquatic environment", *Journal of Hazardous Materials*, Vol. 175/1-3, pp. 45-95, https://doi.org/10.1016/j.jhazmat.2009.10.100. [35]

Schultz, M. et al. (2011), "Selective uptake and biological consequences of environmentally relevant antidepressant pharmaceutical exposures on male fathead minnows", *Aquatic Toxicology*, Vol. 104/1-2, pp. 38-47, https://doi.org/10.1016/j.aquatox.2011.03.011. [71]

SIGRE (2018), *Sustainability Report*, https://www.sigre.es/en/wp-content/uploads/2019/09/SIGRE_Sustainability_Report-2018_Executive_Summary.pdf (accessed on 12 March 2020). [151]

Singrem (2018), *Legal framework and SINGREM statistics*, https://www.singrem.org.mx/marcoLegal.html (accessed on 11 August 2020). [130]

Sirum (2020), *SIRUM – Saving Medicine : Saving Lives*, https://www.sirum.org/ (accessed on 7 October 2020). [101]

Stadt Wien (2022), *Altmedikamente richtig entsorgen*, https://www.wien.gv.at/umwelt/ma48/beratung/muelltrennung/altmedikamente-richtig-entsorgen.html (accessed on 29 April 2022). [139]

State Institute For Drug Control (2007), *Převzetí nepoužitelných léčiv k likvidaci, Státní ústav pro kontrolu léčiv*, http://www.sukl.cz/lekarny/prevzeti-nepouzitelnych-leciv-k-likvidaci (accessed on 12 March 2020). [141]

State institute for drug control (2020), "Disposal of unused drugs by private individuals - Guidance document", https://www.sukl.sk/buxus/docs/Inspekcia/Odpady/MP_105_-_2020_Zneskodnovanie_liekov_nespotrebovanych_fyzickymi_osobami.pdf (accessed on 7 March 2022). [149]

Stoker, T., E. Gibson and L. Zorrilla (2010), "Triclosan exposure modulates estrogen-dependent responses in the female wistar rat", *Toxicological Sciences*, Vol. 117/1, pp. 45-53, https://doi.org/10.1093/toxsci/kfq180. [55]

Sui, Q. et al. (2017), "Pharmaceuticals and personal care products in the leachates from a typical landfill reservoir of municipal solid waste in Shanghai, China: Occurrence and removal by a full-scale membrane bioreactor", *Journal of Hazardous Materials*, Vol. 323, pp. 99-108, https://doi.org/10.1016/j.jhazmat.2016.03.047. [31]

SuperDrecksKëscht (2020), *Medicine - SDK*, https://sdk.lu/en/dictionary/medication-cosmetics-and-medical-waste/ (accessed on 12 March 2020). [146]

Swedish Pharmacy Association (2021), *Sveriges Apoteksföreningen - Annual Report 2021*, http://sverigesapoteksforening.se/wp-content/uploads/2021/05/2021-Annual-Report-1.pdf (accessed on 17 November 2021). [118]

Thomas, K. et al. (2007), "Source to sink tracking of selected human pharmaceuticals from two Oslo city hospitals and a wastewater treatment works", *Journal of Environmental Monitoring*, Vol. 9/12, p. 1410, https://doi.org/10.1039/b709745j. [19]

Tong, A., B. Peake and R. Braund (2011), "Disposal practices for unused medications around the world", *Environment International*, Vol. 37/1, pp. 292-298, https://doi.org/10.1016/j.envint.2010.10.002. [95]

Trueman, P. et al. (2010), *Evaluation of the Scale, Causes and Costs of Waste Medicines*, https://discovery.ucl.ac.uk/id/eprint/1350234/1/Evaluation_of_NHS_Medicines_Waste__web_publication_version.pdf (accessed on 13 February 2020). [15]

Trust for America's Health (2015), *The Facts Hurt: A state-by-state injury prevention policy report*, https://www.tfah.org/report-details/the-facts-hurt-a-state-by-state-injury-prevention-policy-report/#:~:text=Wyoming-,The%20Facts%20Hurt%3A%20A%20State%2DBy%2DState%20Injury%20Prevention,and%20decreased%20in%20nine%20states. (accessed on 24 July 2019). [11]

UBA (2018), *Recommendations for reducing micropollutants in waters*, https://www.umweltbundesamt.de/sites/default/files/medien/1410/publikationen/180709_uba_pos_mikroverunreinigung_en_bf.pdf (accessed on 30 April 2019). [106]

US Government (2010), *An Act To amend the Controlled Substances Act to provide for take-back disposal of controlled substances in certain instances, and for other purposes*, https://www.deadiversion.usdoj.gov/drug_disposal/non_registrant/s_3397.pdf (accessed on 25 February 2020). [157]

VALORMED (2020), *VALORMED apresenta o Relatório de Actividades 2019*, http://www.valormed.pt/article/view/318/valormed-apresenta-o-relatorio-de-actividades-2019 (accessed on 10 August 2020). [131]

Vargas, F. (2018), *A dónde van los residuos farmacéuticos en Chile? - El Mostrador*, https://www.elmostrador.cl/agenda-pais/2018/10/18/a-donde-van-los-residuos-farmaceuticos-en-chile/ (accessed on 12 March 2020). [140]

Vellinga, A. et al. (2014), "Public practice regarding disposal of unused medicines in Ireland", *Science of The Total Environment*, Vol. 478, pp. 98-102, https://doi.org/10.1016/j.scitotenv.2014.01.085. [85]

Vestel, J. et al. (2016), "Use of acute and chronic ecotoxicity data in environmental risk assessment of pharmaceuticals", *Environmental Toxicology and Chemistry*, Vol. 35/5, pp. 1201-1212, https://doi.org/10.1002/etc.3260. [53]

Winning Scientific Management (2018), *Auscultação a utentes e farmácias-Relatório de Resultados*. [92]

World Bank (2018), *What a Waste 2.0 : A Global Snapshot of Solid Waste Management to 2050*, World Bank, Washington, DC: World Bank. [34]

Xia, L., L. Zheng and J. Zhou (2017), "Effects of ibuprofen, diclofenac and paracetamol on hatch and motor behavior in developing zebrafish (Danio rerio)", *Chemosphere*, Vol. 182, pp. 416-425, https://doi.org/10.1016/j.chemosphere.2017.05.054. [39]

ZonMw (2020), *Feasibility of redispensing novel oral anticancer agents unused by patients: the return study*, https://www.zonmw.nl/nl/onderzoek-resultaten/doelmatigheidsonderzoek/programmas/project-detail/goed-gebruik-geneesmiddelen/feasibility-of-redispensing-novel-oral-anticancer-agents-unused-by-patients-the-return-study/verslagen/. [102]

Zounková, R. et al. (2007), "Ecotoxicity and genotoxicity assessment of cytostatic pharmaceuticals", *Environmental Toxicology and Chemistry*, Vol. 26/10, p. 2208, https://doi.org/10.1897/07-137R.1. [46]